# JEFF SMITH

# The
# K.P.I.
# Book

*"The ultimate guide to understanding the Key Performance Indicators of your business"*

# YOURS TO HAVE AND TO HOLD
# BUT NOT TO COPY

© 2001 Insight Training & Development Limited.

This publication is protected by copyright law. All rights are reserved. No portion of this book may be reproduced or used in any form – graphic, electronic or mechanical including photocopying, sound recording, information storage and retrieval systems, or by any other means without the written permission from the publisher.

Published by:

Insight Training & Development Limited
P. O. Box 1234
Stourbridge
England
DY8 2GE

| | |
|---|---|
| Telephone UK: | 01384 371432 |
| International: | 0044 1384 371432 |
| Web Address | www.AskInsight.com |
| Email: | KPI@AskInsight.com |
| | |
| ISBN: | 0-9540259-0-3 |

The right of Jeff Smith to be identified as the author of this work has been asserted by him in accordance with the Copyright, Designs and Patents Act 1988.

First printed in the UK 2001 by:
RPM Reprographics Chichester.

Dedicated to my three girls.
Sharon, Sophie and Lara

I love you more than anything.

# Acknowledgements

I am in the very privileged position of meeting and working with many dedicated and talented people who continue to pass on, and share their knowledge with me. If I have excelled in this industry it is because I have been standing on the shoulders of giants.

I have taken so much from the motor industry, for which I shall be eternally grateful; this book is one way to give something back in return. It's my way of giving back to the industry what so many people ask me for everyday, help with the understanding of their business.

This book could never have been written without the support and co-operation of many of my friends, clients and colleagues who have put up with my incessant badgering in the pursuit of obtaining accuracy and clarification of the Key Performance Indicators of our industry. Your advice and support has been invaluable.

***Special thanks*** go to Professor Garel Rhys OBE for believing in my work. I am *honoured* that you have chosen to write the Foreword which gives us all such a clear insight into the issues of the present and future of our industry.

***Extra-special thanks*** go to my wife Sharon for your unerring confidence in my ability to bring this project to life. I know that you have made many sacrifices to provide me with the time to write this book; I don't know what I've done to deserve you, I feel truly blessed to have you in my life.

*Thank you.*

# About The Author

Jeff Smith is regarded by many as one of the UK's leading business improvement strategists. He is particularly well known for his ability to convey complex information into jargon busting, plain English that everyone understands. As well as being one of the motor industry's top trainers and consultants, he is also a founder member of the Professional Speakers Association and has appeared many times as a motor industry expert on Sky Television.

Jeff's career spans 20 years within the motor industry. He has progressed through the Sales Department to become Dealer Principal and then to Divisional Director within a retail motor group.

He followed this by becoming a Consultant to the Motor Industry and during this time he's worked with many manufacturers developing their profit improvement programmes within Sales, Aftersales and Business Management for Dealer Principals and Line Managers.

As well as speaking at conferences and product launches around the world, Jeff continues to work with manufacturers developing training courses for their dealer networks and he also runs open training courses and bespoke in-house coaching programmes for individual dealerships and major groups.

You are welcome to contact him directly by email on JeffSmith@AskInsight.com

# Foreword
*By Professor Garel Rhys OBE*

Training and education are the foundation of the success and competitiveness of companies in a modern high wage economy. Together they ensure the development and use of best practice that in turn generates low unit cost operations. This is particularly so in the automotive sector in general and the retail segment of the industry in particular.

The retail motor industry will only be taken seriously as an economic activity and as a worthwhile high status career if the competence of those working within it is of a universally high level. It is no wonder that unease exists about the quality of the sector when someone could be selling fast foods in the high street one week, and set loose in a retail dealership to sell expensive motor cars the next. Vehicle retailing and service is a highly complex and demanding business which is facing an ever more expert clientele armed with more and more information. In order to bring value added to the process the "operators" in vehicle retailing and service, new and used, from top executive to junior sales men and women and mechanic must display a thorough understanding of the nature of the business they are in. The customers expect no less.

Central to this is knowledge of the financials of business and the areas in which they apply. This volume is an excellent way of doing this. It does not hesitate to tackle issues head on, and the result is a straightforward way of illuminating complex issues with a focused and clear light.

To those who felt that the financial issues confronting business were beyond their understanding, or of no relevance to them, will find on reading this book that this is no longer so.

In the USA when there is a hint of economic trouble, industry increases its training budget to improve the knowledge base of its workforce so that it will deal better with challenges. This must become the approach in the UK and especially in the motor retail and sales sector.

The "goodies" to be found in this volume should stimulate excitement: the excitement that follows really understanding important concepts and seeing their relevance and importance.


**Professor Garel Rhys OBE**
Director of the Centre for Automotive Industry Research
Cardiff University Business School

*"Understanding the practical structure as well as
the financial structure of your business
is inseparable from your ability
to influence its profitability"*

*Jeff Smith*

# Contents

| | |
|---|---|
| **Introduction** | 11 |
| **How to use this book** | 12 |
| **Interpreting your Sales Department** | 19 |
| Typical Sales Department Structure | 20 |
| % Value of Stock Over 90 days | 21 |
| Adopted Stock | 22 |
| Advertising Cost per Unit Sold | 23 |
| Annualised Sales | 24 |
| Annualised Sales per Salesperson | 25 |
| Average Selling Price | 26 |
| Cost of Overage Stock (Used Vehicles) | 27 |
| Days Supply (New Vehicles) | 28 |
| Days Supply (Used Vehicles) | 29 |
| Departmental Expenses | 30 |
| Departmental Profit % | 31 |
| Direct Expenses | 32 |
| Direct Profit % | 33 |
| Finance Commission per Unit | 34 |
| Finance Penetration | 35 |
| Gross Profit – New Vehicles | 36 |
| Gross Profit - Used Vehicles | 37 |
| Lost Opportunity Costs (Used Vehicles) | 38 |
| New:Used Retail Ratio | 39 |

| | |
|---|---|
| Operating Profit % | 40 |
| Other Income | 41 |
| Policy Costs | 42 |
| Reconditioning Costs | 43 |
| Rectification | 44 |
| Retail:Trade Used Ratio | 45 |
| Return on Investment (Used Vehicles) | 46 |
| Sales Commissions | 47 |
| Semi-Fixed Expenses | 48 |
| Stock Turn (Version 1) | 49 |
| Stock Turn (Version 2) | 50 |
| Stock Turn (Days, Used Vehicles) | 51 |
| Target Related Bonus | 52 |
| Used:New Retail Ratio | 53 |
| Used Vehicle Stock Ageing | 54 |
| Used Vehicle Stocking Plan | 55 |
| Used Vehicle Stock Value | 56 |
| Used Vehicle Write Down | 57 |
| Variable Expenses | 58 |
| Vehicle Debtor Days | 59 |

| | |
|---|---|
| **Interpreting your Service Department** | 61 |
| Typical Service Department Structure | 62 |
| Debtor Days | 63 |
| Departmental Expenses | 64 |
| Departmental Profit % | 65 |
| Direct Expenses | 66 |
| Direct Profit % | 67 |
| Diverted Time | 68 |
| Gross Profit % | 69 |
| Hours Attended | 70 |
| Hours Bought | 71 |
| Hours per Parc | 72 |
| Hours per Retail Job Card | 73 |
| Hours Sold | 74 |
| Hours Worked | 75 |
| Idle Time | 76 |
| Labour Cost of Sales | 77 |
| Labour Efficiency % | 78 |
| Labour Gross Profit | 79 |
| Labour Gross Profit % | 80 |
| Labour Sales Mix | 81 |
| Labour Utilisation % | 82 |
| Lead Time | 83 |
| Lost Time | 84 |

| | |
|---|---:|
| Oil & Lubricants Profitability | 85 |
| Operating Profit % | 86 |
| Overall Efficiency % | 87 |
| Parts Sales per Labour Hour | 88 |
| Policy Costs | 89 |
| Productive Efficiency % | 90 |
| Productive Ratio | 91 |
| Productivity % | 92 |
| Productive Staff : Non-Productive Staff | 93 |
| Recovery Rate | 94 |
| Rectification | 95 |
| Repair Orders per Technician | 96 |
| Retail : Internal Ratio | 97 |
| Revenue per Technician | 98 |
| Selling Efficiency % | 99 |
| Semi-Fixed Expenses | 100 |
| Service Sales per Parc Unit | 101 |
| Sub Contract Profitability | 102 |
| Utilisation % | 103 |
| Variable Expenses | 104 |
| Vehicle Parc | 105 |
| Working Efficiency % | 106 |
| Work-In-Progress (Days) | 107 |

| | |
|---|---|
| **Interpreting your Parts Department** | 109 |
| Typical Parts Department Structure | 110 |
| Annualised Parts Sales | 111 |
| Average Bought Cost | 112 |
| Average Buying Margin % | 113 |
| Debtor Days | 114 |
| Departmental Expenses | 115 |
| Departmental Profit | 116 |
| Direct Expenses | 117 |
| Direct Profit | 118 |
| Emergency Order % | 119 |
| Oil & Lubricants Profitability | 120 |
| Operating Profit | 121 |
| Obsolete Stock | 122 |
| Parts Gross Profit | 123 |
| Parts Gross Profit % | 124 |
| Parts Net Profit per New Unit Sold | 125 |
| Parts Sales | 126 |
| Parts Sales Mix | 127 |
| Parts Sales per Parc Unit | 128 |
| Parts Stock Value | 129 |
| Parts Sales Per Employee | 130 |
| Rebates and Bonuses | 131 |
| Semi-Fixed Expenses | 132 |

| | |
|---|---|
| Stock Adjustments | 133 |
| Total Parts Stock Turn | 134 |
| True Parts Stock Turn *(Version 1)* | 135 |
| True Parts Stock Turn *(Version 2)* | 136 |
| V.O.R % *(Version 1)* | 137 |
| V.O.R % *(Version 2)* | 138 |
| V.O.R. Penalty | 139 |
| V.O.R. Penalty % | 140 |

| | |
|---|---|
| **Interpreting your Bodyshop** | 141 |
| Typical Bodyshop Structure | 142 |
| Debtor Days | 143 |
| Departmental Expenses | 144 |
| Departmental Profit % | 145 |
| Direct Expenses | 146 |
| Direct Profit % | 147 |
| Diverted Time | 148 |
| Estimate Conversion Ratio | 149 |
| Gross Profit % | 150 |
| Hours Attended | 151 |
| Hours Bought | 152 |
| Hours per Vehicle Parc | 153 |
| Hours Sold | 154 |
| Hours Sold per Repair | 155 |
| Hours Worked | 156 |
| Idle Time | 157 |
| Labour Cost of Sales | 158 |
| Labour Efficiency % | 159 |
| Labour Gross Profit | 160 |
| Labour Gross Profit % | 161 |
| Labour Sales per Parc Unit | 162 |
| Labour Sales Mix | 163 |
| Labour Utilisation % | 164 |

| | |
|---|---|
| Lead Time | 165 |
| Lost Time | 166 |
| Operating Profit % | 167 |
| Overall Efficiency % | 168 |
| Paint & Materials per Labour Hour | 169 |
| Parts Sales per Labour Hour | 170 |
| Policy Costs | 171 |
| Productive Efficiency % | 172 |
| Productive Ratio | 173 |
| Productivity % | 174 |
| Productive Staff : Non-Productive Staff | 175 |
| Recovery Rate | 176 |
| Rectification | 177 |
| Repair Orders per Productive | 178 |
| Retail : Insurance Ratio | 179 |
| Revenue per Productive | 180 |
| Selling Efficiency % | 181 |
| Semi-Fixed Expenses | 182 |
| Utilisation % | 183 |
| Variable Expenses | 184 |
| Vehicle Parc | 185 |
| Working Efficiency % | 186 |
| Work-In-Progress (Days) | 187 |

**Interpreting your Business Information** 189
Absorption % *(Version 1)* 190
Absorption % *(Version 2)* 191
Acid Test *(Version 1)* 192
Acid Test *(Version 2)* 193
Breakeven Volume 194
Capital Employed 195
Cash Profits 196
Circulation of Current Assets (C.O.C.A.) 197
Circulation of Funds Employed (C.O.F.E.) 198
Current Ratio 199
Debtor Creditor Ratio 200
Debtor Days 201
Debt Equity Ratio 202
Equity % 203
Fixed Asset % 204
Funds Employed 205
Gearing Ratio 206
Gearing % 207
Interest % 208
Interest Cover 209
Investment 210
Loan Repayment % 211
Net Profit After Interest % (N.P.A.I.) 212

| | |
|---|---|
| Net Profit Before Interest % (N.P.B.I.) | 213 |
| Net Profit Before Tax % (N.P.B.T.) | 214 |
| Return on Funds Employed % (R.O.F.E.) | 215 |
| Return on Investment % (R.O.I.) | 216 |
| Return on Net Worth | 217 |
| Return on Own Funds | 218 |
| Return on Sales % (R.O.S.) | 219 |
| Working Capital | 220 |
| Working Capital Ratio | 221 |
| **Conclusion** | 223 |
| **How to order additional copies** | 225 |

# Introduction

There are around two hundred K.P.I's currently in use within the motor industry and to operate your business effectively, you are expected to understand them all.

Most people do not work with K.P.I's every single day and because of this fact, you need a simple and effective reminder of their meanings so that you can correctly interpret your dealership information.

This book has been written because everyone who works with Key Performance Indicators needs a central point of reference. Something that gives you the information that you want with complete understanding in less than two minutes.

Your management accounts, franchise composite reports and daily operating controls offer a wealth of information but it is the K.P.I's that derive from these sources of information that yield the real power of understanding.

This book removes the mystique that often surrounds K.P.I's so that you can better interpret your dealership information, and with this clarity of understanding you will be unlocking your true potential to achieve greater results on a consistent basis.

The quality and size of this book has been designed so that it fits snugly in to your briefcase providing you with the constant source of reference that you will draw upon for the rest of your career.

# How To Use This Book

One of the biggest benefits that you will find from using this book is that you don't have to make time to read it. What I mean by this is that you can access the information very quickly and gain understanding without reading through countless pages of other information to get to the part that you really want.

This has been achieved by ensuring that the explanation of each Key Performance Indicator is condensed to one single page, thereby ensuring that you gain complete understanding in less than two minutes in most cases.

To ensure your ease of reference, as well as comprehensive indexing, the book has been divided into five separate sections, which of course represent five different parts of your dealership.

These five divisions are Sales Department, Service Department, Parts Department, Bodyshop and Business Management. Within each of these sections you will find all of the K.P.I's that you need, listed in alphabetical order.

At the top of the page, the first thing that you will see is the name of the Key Performance Indicator printed in bold letters.

Underneath the name of the Key Performance Indicator you will see the mathematical formula that is used for its calculation.

Beneath this mathematical formula you will see one of three words together with a corresponding statistic. The three words used here are **Benchmark**, **Baseline**, or **Guideline**.

Key Performance Indicators provide you with meaningful statistics about the direction and travel of your business. In some cases it is possible to state how a particular Key Performance Indicator should behave, or in other words we can state what result should be generated to ensure optimum performance in a given area.

Generally speaking, the term that is used throughout the industry for these optimal levels of best practise is the word Benchmark. In my own experience this term is very useful for keeping performance *constrained* at a specific level and because of this it brings with it some psychological limitations in the area of dealership profitability.

Because of these implications I have introduced an additional term, which I call a Baseline. My aim in introducing this term is to remove any limitations that may exist when dealing with Profitability. Here are my own definitions of these two main terms:

**Benchmark.**
This term is used when your performance is to be maintained at a specific level or it is to operate within an upper or lower limit. For example, Utilisation within the Service Department should not be any lower than 85% nor should it be any higher than 95%. These two parameters represent the Benchmark within which Utilisation should be performing.

When used in this context, the term Benchmark is useful for constraining performance because the manager reading this statistic usually thinks that this area has reached its Benchmark and therefore everything is performing as it should be. However, this mindset produces a limiting factor when dealing with issues of profitability. This is because a manager might elevate their performance in an area such as Gross Profit to reach a particular Benchmark and then stop any further development because they have reached the required level, or in other words, they may think that the Benchmark is the only place to be.

**Baseline**
This term is used when you want to express a starting point for a given area of performance. This is not the place to be, it is a minimum expectation.

A Benchmark suggests that you should reach a given level of performance and maintain it. A Baseline suggests that you should reach a given level of performance as an absolute minimum and you should continue to develop the area.

Baselines are particularly useful when setting objectives in all levels of profitability because they do not have the limiting factor of setting an upper limit at which many people may stop any further development.

Care should be taken when measuring performance against both Benchmarks and Baselines as people have a tendency to aspire to what is expected of them and it is therefore of vital importance that you convey your expectations when constructing budgets and business plans.

**Guideline**
This term is used when a Benchmark or Baseline cannot be applied to a specific area of performance. For example, Reconditioning Costs on used vehicles vary greatly from franchise to franchise. For some, the figure could be £200 per unit and for others it could be £1200. In this instance the Guideline will read Franchise Specific.

When you have read the main title, mathematical formula, the Benchmark, Baseline or Guideline, you will reach the main body of the text.

The first few lines of this text set out to explain exactly what the Key Performance Indicator is measuring. It will also inform you of any alternative name by which this Key Performance Indicator is known.

For example, Utilisation within the Service Department is also known as Labour Efficiency. To avoid any confusion, both of these terms are listed within the Service Department, both of them refer to each other, and both carry exactly the same explanation.

Also contained within the main text of the page is a working example that explains the Key Performance Indicator at its most basic level to ensure complete understanding.

In some explanations, other Key Performance Indicators are mentioned. Where this is the case, these words are capitalised, which means that the relevant K.P.I. is also listed within the book carrying a detailed explanation.

You know by now that the letters K.P.I represent the words Key Performance Indicators, but what about the letters K.P.S. and K.P.A? Firstly, let's deal with K.P.A.

**K.P.A.**
These letters represent the words **Key Performance Area**. Typically, a K.P.A. refers to a general area of your business as opposed to an isolated piece of information. For example, used vehicles may be a Key Performance Area that you may wish to focus upon and within this area there are many different isolated performance criteria. Generally speaking, a K.P.A. is a grouping of information as opposed to focussing on an individual item.

**K.P.S.**
These letters represent the words **Key Performance Standard**. Typically a K.P.S. is much the same as a Benchmark, or in other words they set the standard for a given level of performance. For instance, some people may say that they are hoping to achieve a Used Vehicle Stock Turn of 10 times per annum. This figure represents their target or in other words their Key Performance Standard.

I have chosen to steer away form using the term K.P.S. because in some instances it may carry with it the same limitations as the term Benchmark.

If you applied a Key Performance Standard of 8 times a year for Stock Turn on used vehicles, some people may think that the word standard suggests that this is the place to be rather than just a starting point. Throughout this book the term K.P.S. has been replaced with the terms Benchmark or Baseline.

## K.P.I.

This section of the book would not be complete without a description of the term Key Performance Indicator, so here is my own definition.

A Key Performance Indicator breaks down all areas of your business into single bite-sized chunks that are much easier to manage. They help to remove the emotion away from vehicles and get you focussed on the thing that your job is really about, which is making money.

As an industry, we produce Management Accounts and Composite reports that are intricately detailed and extremely comprehensive. It is in fact fair to say that the management information that is produced by the motor industry is, in many cases, far superior to many other industries. This complexity has not happened by accident, their evolution has become critical in measuring dealership performance, purely for means of our survival.

The downside to comprehensive Management Accounts is that you have to take time to read them, and it is often difficult to get away from the emotion of the millions of pounds of turnover and thousands of pounds of profit. Key Performance Indicators on the other hand are much more static and stable and therefore carry more meaning when comparing information.

As with all information, the best way of understanding it is to track or trend its performance. The K.P.I. tells you where performance has been in the past, where it is now, and perhaps more useful, where performance is likely to be in the future.

K.P.I's really are fabulous tools for measuring and comparing your performance with others. However, the downside is that some K.P.I's mean different things to different people and many comparisons are rendered meaningless because different criteria are being used as well as different names. Frankly, it can get confusing!

My aims in writing this book are twofold, the first being to eradicate all confusion surrounding the interpretation and calculation of K.P.I's so that a common dialogue can be established at your business meetings. My second aim is to produce a reference manual that will aid and speed up your development within the motor industry. I hope you find it useful.

# Interpreting Your Sales Department

**Top K.P.I's to study:**

**Stock Turn
Direct Expenses
Reconditioning Costs**

# Typical Sales Department Structure

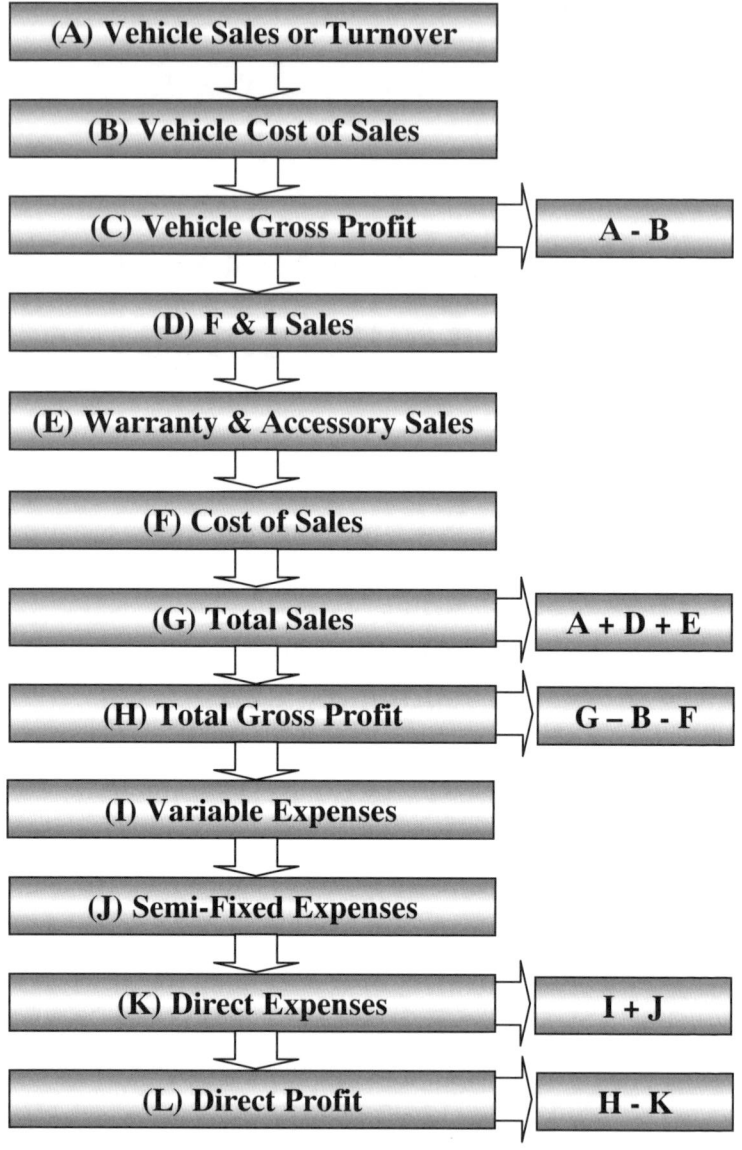

# % Value of Stock Over 90 days

## Value of Stock Over 90 days ÷ Stock Value (x 100)

## Benchmark: < 10% of Stock Value

This K.P.I. takes the total value of your used vehicle stock, and then states the collective value of the vehicles that are over 90 days old as a percentage of the total value. In other words, if you have £250,000 invested in used vehicles, how much of this money is invested in vehicles that have been in stock for more than 90 days?

Example:
(A) Value of Stock Over 90 Days  = £17,500
(B) Value of Total Used Stock    = £250,000
(C) **% of Funds Over 90 days**  = 7% (A ÷ B x 100)

This K.P.I. very wisely moves away from used vehicle units and measures the money that is invested within them.

The example above illustrates that 7% of the money that is invested in used vehicle stock is currently invested in used vehicles that have been in stock for more than 90 days. What the K.P.I. does not tell you is how much longer than 90 days has the investment been there.

This is a very useful trend to assess because it measures the ability to manage the money that is invested in used vehicle stock as opposed to the units themselves.

It removes the emotion that is often attached to those used vehicles that someone will buy one day, and focuses your mind on the real issue at stake: Money.

# Adopted Stock

## Fully Paid New Vehicle Stock

### Benchmark: 0

Most new vehicle stock is supplied to a dealer from a franchise manufacturer on a consignment basis. This means that when new vehicles are delivered, the dealer usually pays the interest charges or stocking charges as they are more commonly known.

After an defined period (typically 120 days) the new vehicles have to be adopted by the dealer, or in other words, the dealer must pay for the vehicles in full.

Before reaching the point of adoption, when a dealer sells a vehicle, the consignment agreement stipulates that the vehicle must be paid for at the point of registration. Therefore new vehicle stock is paid in full in one of two scenarios.

1) When the vehicles are registered
2) When they reach the end of the consignment period

When vehicles reach the end of their consignment period they become Adopted Stock. The worst scenario that can happen is to be adopting vehicles because it absorbs huge amounts of money, which in turn prevents activity in other areas of your business.

It is therefore in your interest to sell all new vehicles prior to any of them becoming Adopted Stock.

# Advertising Cost per Unit Sold

## £ Spent on Advertising ÷ Units Sold

## Guideline: Own Policy

This K.P.I establishes the average amount of money that has been spent per unit sold. Beware! This is definitely <u>not</u> a measurement of your advertising effectiveness.

Example:
(A) Money Spent on Advertising       = £84,201
(B) Units Sold                       = 663
(C) **£ Advertising per Unit Sold**  = **£127** (A ÷ B)

Firstly, the units sold should relate only to retail units and ideally, you should have a separate K.P.I for new and used vehicles.

This statistic is influenced by many factors, not least of which being the selling skills of your sales team. You could produce a fantastic advertisement that produces lots of enquiries and for one reason or another your sales team fail to convert them into sales.

This result would generate a high advertising spend per unit sold which could lead you to the false conclusion that that you are spending too much on advertising.

This K.P.I. is useful for ascertaining your advertising budget for retail sales, based on your sales objectives and should not be used to judge advertising effectiveness.

*Advertising Effectiveness is covered in great detail in the next book in this series.*

# Annualised Sales

## Projected Annual Sales Volume

## Guideline: Own Policy

In order to calculate many Key Performance Indicators, your vehicle Sales Volume may need to be annualised. This is simply a projection of your annual sales based on your current sales performance.

The formula is the year-to-date sales volume figure, multiplied by 12 then divided by the current month number. For example, if your current reporting period is January to April year-to-date, then the sales figure is multiplied by 12 (12 months in 1 year) and then divided by 4 (April is the $4^{th}$ month in your reporting period).

Example:
(A) January Sales = 58
(B) February Sales = 43
(C) March Sales = 79
(D) April Sales = 45
(E) Sales to date = 225
(F) Multiply by 12 = 2,700
(G) Divide by current month = 4 (April)
(H) **Annualised Sales** = **675**   (F ÷ G)

This is a theoretical figure that provides you with the Sales volume that you will achieve at the end of the year if your sales performance where to be maintained at the current rate.

This method of calculating Annualised Sales is used in many Key Performance Indicators.

# Annualised Sales per Salesperson

## Annualised Unit Sales ÷ Number of Sales People

### Baseline: > 150 units per annum

This K.P.I simply measures the average number of units a Salesperson sells in 1 year.

Example:
(A) Annualised Sales = 945
(B) Number of Salespeople = 5
(C) **Sales per Salesperson = 189** (A ÷ B)

This statistic provides you with your average sales team performance and you may wish to conduct the same formula for each member of the team to accurately assess the strengths and weaknesses. To achieve this result, see Annualised Sales on the previous page, do the calculation for each Salesperson, and there you have it.

It is generally accepted that a newcomer to the industry will sell around 150 units per annum and a good, well-established Salesperson will sell in excess of 200 units per annum with average performers anywhere between the two.

# Average Selling Price

## Sales Value of Units Sold ÷ Number of Units Sold

## Guideline: Own Policy

This K.P.I applies to both new and used vehicles and provides you with your average selling price of the vehicles that you have sold.

Example:
(A) Invoice value of vehicles sold = £11,776,590
(B) Number of units sold = 945
(C) **Average Selling Price** = **£12,462** (A ÷ B)

This statistic is usually provided for you on your franchise manufacturers composite reports and shows the average selling price for new and used vehicles separately.

It is useful for establishing your funding requirements in stock when you are putting together your budgets and business plans.

It is also useful in the assessment of your stock profiling exercises for used vehicles whilst your figures for the new vehicles will be heavily influenced by your fleet sales activity and your customer profile.

# Cost of Overage Stock *(Used Vehicles)*

## Days in stock ÷ Days Stock Turn x GP per Unit

## Benchmark: < Gross Profit per Unit x 2

This statistic measures the profitability of the space that a used vehicle occupies rather than any measurement of the used vehicle itself. Understanding of this difference is critical to this concept.

Let's assume that your used vehicle Stock Turn is 35 days and your Gross Profit is £1,500 per used vehicle.

If you have a used vehicle that remains in stock for a period of longer than 35 days, then the space it occupies is no longer productive at the average rate and is missing profit opportunities.

In order to establish the value of this lost opportunity you must divide the actual number of days a vehicle has been in stock by your Stock Turn and then multiply this by your average Gross Profit.

Example:
(A) Actual Days in Stock = 87
(B) Stock Turn = 35 Days
(C) Failed to sell = 2.49 times (A ÷ B)
(D) Average Gross Profit = £1,500
(E) **Cost of Overage Stock** = **£3,735** (C x D)

This concept accepts the principle that your used vehicles generate £1,500 every 35 days, whereas this vehicle has failed to do so 2.49 times.

# Days Supply *(New Vehicles)*

## Days in Period ÷ Sales:Stock Ratio

## Guideline: Franchise Specific

This K.P.I aims to calculate how many days of new vehicle supply you currently have in stock.

Example:
(A) Days in Period = 90
(B) Units Sold = 39
(C) Units in Stock = 21
(D) Sales:Stock Ratio = 1.86 (B ÷ C)
(E) **Days Supply** = **48 days** (A ÷ D)

This illustration is showing that if you carry on selling at your current Sales:Stock ratio, then you have enough stock to continue trading for 48 days.

Vehicle supply varies considerably between franchise manufacturers, which is the main influence on this Key Performance Indicator.

# Days Supply *(Used Vehicles)*

## 365 ÷ Stock Turn (Annual)

## Baseline: < 45 Days

This is also known as Days Stock Turn. This K.P.I aims to calculate how many days of vehicle supply you are currently working with.

Example:
(A) Number of days in 1 year = 365
(B) Annual Stock Turn = 10.4
(C) **Days Supply** = **35 days** (A ÷ B)

This illustration is showing that if you carry on selling at your current sales rate, then you have enough stock to continue trading for 35 days.

Obviously, you do not need to carry any more stock than is absolutely necessary because that would be a total waste of your money.

When dealing with used vehicles, you need to read this page in conjunction with Stock Turn to determine the performance that you require.

# Departmental Expenses

## Departmental Expenses ÷ Turnover (x100)

### Guideline: Franchise Specific

The Departmental Expenses of the Sales Department are also know as Direct Expenses and refer to the total expenses incurred. They represent the sum total of the Variable Expenses and Semi-Fixed Expenses.

Typically, Departmental Expenses are shown as a monetary value and in order for you to capture meaningful trend analysis you will need to express them as a percentage of departmental Turnover.

Example:
(A) Variable Expenses = £133,778
(B) Semi-Fixed Expenses = £280,326
(C) **Departmental Expenses** = **£414,104** (A + B)
(D) Department Turnover = £7,432,165
(E) Vehicles Sold = 784
(F) Total Expenses p/unit = £528 (C ÷ E)
(G) **Departmental Expense %** = **5.57%** (C ÷ D x 100)

Keeping control of Departmental Expenses can be a difficult task unless you fully understand the difference between Variable Expenses and Semi-Fixed Expenses.

Variable Expenses are directly linked to sales volume and Semi-Fixed Expenses are not linked to sales volume therefore the actions that you need to take to maintain control is different in each area.

# Departmental Profit %

## Departmental Profit ÷ Turnover (x100)

## Guideline: Franchise Specific

The Departmental Profit of the Sales Department is also called many other things such as, Direct Profit, Operating Profit and of course the bottom line.

Departmental Profit is calculated by taking Gross Profit minus Departmental Expenses. To make sense of this figure it is always expressed as a percentage of Turnover when used for trending as it is the direction of travel that is of most interest to you.

Example:
(A) Departmental Profit     =  £97,208
(B) Departmental Turnover   =  £3,240,233
(C) **Departmental Profit %  =  3%**   (A ÷ B x 100)

Keeping track of your Departmental Profit % is best shown in the form of a simple graph that is updated monthly so that you can see the trends that are emerging.

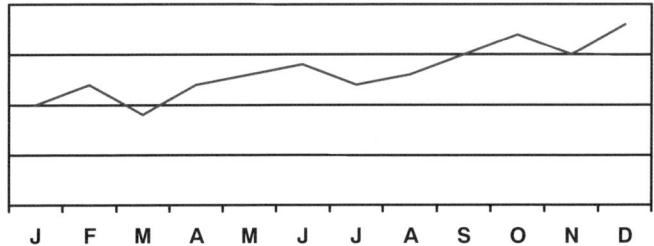

# Direct Expenses

## Direct Expenses ÷ Turnover (x100)

## Guideline: Franchise Specific

The Direct Expenses of the Sales Department are also know as Departmental Expenses and refer to the total expenses incurred. They represent the sum total of the Variable Expenses and Semi-Fixed Expenses.

Typically, Direct Expenses are shown as a monetary value and in order for you to capture meaningful trend analysis you will need to express them as a percentage of departmental Turnover.

Example:
(A) Variable Expenses = £133,778
(B) Semi-Fixed Expenses = £280,326
(C) **Direct Expenses** = **£414,104** (A + B)
(D) Department Turnover = £7,432,165
(E) Vehicles Sold = 784
(F) Direct Expenses p/unit = £528 (C ÷ E)
(G) **Direct Expense %** = **3.7%** (C ÷ D x 100)

Keeping control of Direct Expenses can be a difficult task unless you fully understand the difference between Variable Expenses and Semi-Fixed Expenses.

Variable Expenses are directly linked to sales volume and Semi-Fixed Expenses are not linked to sales volume therefore the actions that you need to take to maintain control is different in each area.

# Direct Profit %

## Direct Profit ÷ Turnover (x100)

## Guideline: Franchise Specific

The Direct Profit of the Sales Department is also called many other things such as, Departmental Profit, Operating Profit and of course the bottom line.

Direct Profit is calculated by taking Gross Profit minus Departmental Expenses. To make sense of this figure it is always expressed as a percentage of Turnover when used for trending as it is the direction of travel that is of most interest to you.

Example:
(A) Direct Profit = £97,208
(B) Departmental Turnover = £3,240,233
(C) **Direct Profit %** = **3%**  (A ÷ B x 100)

Keeping track of your Direct Profit % is best shown in the form of a simple graph that is updated monthly so that you can see the trends that are emerging.

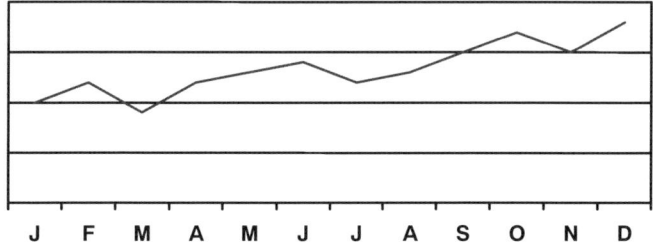

# Finance Commission per Unit

## Finance Commission Earned ÷ Units Sold on Finance

## Guideline: Own Policy

This K.P.I. establishes the average amount of finance commission that you have earned on each unit that you have sold on finance.

Example:
(A) Finance Commission earned = £120,782
(B) Units Sold on Finance = 461
(C) **Finance Commission per Unit** = **£262** (A ÷ B)

The value of commission earned varies significantly between new and used vehicles due to the special subsidised rates offered by franchised manufacturers therefore this K.P.I. is more useful when new and used finance commission is shown separately.

Another factor of high influence is of course a Business Manager, who in many instances will be selling Protected Payment Plans and Gap Insurance to produce much higher levels of finance commission.

You should check your own statistics to ascertain whether or not volume bonus is included in this figure along with the profit generated from warranty as these two factors often cause distortion.

You should also ascertain the units by which the commission is divided. The example shows only the units sold on finance, whereas some reports may divide the commission by every unit sold.

# Finance Penetration

## Total Units Sold ÷ Units Sold on Finance (x 100)

### Baseline: > 30%

This K.P.I establishes the percentage of vehicles that you have sold that have been purchased on finance that has been supplied by your dealership.

Example:
(A) Units Sold on Finance  = 461
(B) Total Units Sold  = 960
(C) **Finance Penetration** = **48.02%**  (A ÷ B x 100)

This example shows that 48% of the vehicles sold were purchased on finance. However, the important thing to note here is the classification of total vehicles sold.

If this statistic is to have any real meaning, then it is only retail sales that should be counted and any fleet sales should be excluded. Before you jump to any conclusions, be certain of the formula of your own K.P.I.

Results also vary between new and used vehicles due to franchise manufacturers sub-vented finance schemes or other attractive offers for new vehicles, therefore this K.P.I. is more useful when new and used finance penetration is shown separately.

The suggested baseline of 30% should be increased to a minimum of 60% were a Business Manager is employed.

# Gross Profit *(New Vehicles)*

## Invoice Price of Vehicle - Cost Price of Vehicle

## Guideline: Franchise Specific

The basic understanding of Gross Profit is simply sales less the cost of those sales. Within the Sales Department there are many things that are sold that are all contained on the sales invoice such as accessories, warranty and of course the vehicle itself.

Take care to understand exactly what your reports are including and excluding from this equation. Generally speaking, most reports will show all of these items separately, especially the Gross Profit in the vehicle.

Example:
(A) Vehicle Sale Price     = £18,268
(B) Vehicle Cost Price     = £17,719
(C) Vehicle Gross Profit   = £549      (A – B)
(D) **Gross Profit %**     = **3%**    (C ÷ A x 100)

There is no benchmark for this K.P.I. because profit retention is very different in all vehicle marques. There is however, one item that needs to be quantified.

When your franchise manufacturer provides you with a tactical bonus payment, is this bonus included or excluded from the vehicle Gross Profit? Also see Target Related Bonus.

The reality is that there is no hard and fast rule for this one and therefore you will need to research your own reports before you draw any conclusions on your results.

# Gross Profit *(Used Vehicles)*

## Invoice Price of Vehicle - S.I.V. of Vehicle

## Baseline: > 10% of Invoice Price

This K.P.I. establishes the amount of Gross Profit that you retain in your used vehicles, this is usually after the deduction of V.A.T. where applicable and before any expenses such as Reconditioning Costs and Sales Commission payments are taken into account.

Example:
(A) Vehicle Sale Price     = £14,500
(B) Vehicle S.I.V.         = £12,679
(C) *Vehicle Gross Profit  = £1,821      (A – B)
(D) **Gross Profit %**     = **12.56%**  (C ÷ A x 100)

The price that you paid for the vehicle may not be the same as the stand in value (S.I.V.) due to the Write Down and write back policies and procedures of your business.

In any event, the value of Gross Profit that you retain from your used vehicles should be greater than 10% of the invoice price. (Not to be confused with the display price on the windscreen)

You need to retain sufficient margin here to pay for all of the Variable and Semi-Fixed Expenses and still have enough left over to make a contribution to Direct Profit.

*Special Note:
This book makes no attempt to cover any regulations surrounding V.A.T. or any other taxation. Please refer to Customs & Excise for guidance.

# Lost Opportunity Costs *(Used Vehicles)*

## Days in Stock ÷ Days Stock Turn x GP per Unit

## Benchmark: < Gross Profit per Unit x 2

This statistic measures the profitability of the space that a used vehicle occupies rather than any measurement of the used vehicle itself. Understanding of this difference is critical to this concept.

Let's assume that your used vehicle Stock Turn is 35 days and your Gross Profit is £1,500 per used vehicle.

If you have a used vehicle that remains in stock for a period of longer than 35 days, then the space it occupies is no longer productive at the average rate and is missing profit opportunities.

In order to establish the value of this lost opportunity you must divide the actual number of days a vehicle has been in stock by your Stock Turn and then multiply this by your average Gross Profit.

Example:
(A) Actual Days in Stock = 87
(B) Current Stock Turn = 35 Days
(C) Failed to sell = 2.49 times (A ÷ B)
(D) Average Gross Profit = £1,500
(E) **Lost Opportunity Cost = £3,735** (C x D)

This concept accepts the principle that your used vehicles generate £1,500 every 35 days, whereas this vehicle has failed to do so 2.49 times therefore the profit opportunity of £3,735 has been lost.

# New:Used Retail Ratio

## New Retail Units Sold ÷ Used Retail Units Sold

### Benchmark: < 1:1

This K.P.I is specifically for retail vehicles and excludes all fleet sales. The statistic establishes the relationship between the number of new vehicles that you retail and the number of used vehicles that you retail.

Example:
(A) New Retail Sales     = 548
(B) Used Retail Sales    = 960
(C) **New :Used Retail Ratio =  0.57:1**  (A ÷ B)

This example shows that for every used vehicle that you retail, you sell 0.57 new retail vehicles. Take the time to understand what you are reading on your reports as some manufacturers calculate this ratio in reverse. (Used: New)

It is not possible to provide an industry benchmark for this performance as it is influenced by the franchise that you operate, your overall trading strategy, the ability of the Sales Manager and the sales team.

# Operating Profit %

## Operating Profit ÷ Department Turnover (x100)

## Guideline: Franchise Specific

The Operating Profit of the Sales Department is also called many other things such as, Departmental Profit, Direct Profit and of course the bottom line.

Operating Profit is calculated by taking Gross Profit minus Departmental Expenses. To make sense of this figure it is always expressed as a percentage of Turnover when used for trending as it is the direction of travel that is of most interest to you.

Example:
(A) Operating Profit = £97,208
(B) Departmental Turnover = £3,240,233
(C) **Operating Profit %** = **3%**   (A ÷ B x 100)

Keeping track of your Operating Profit % is best shown in the form of a simple graph that is updated monthly so that you can see the trends that are emerging.

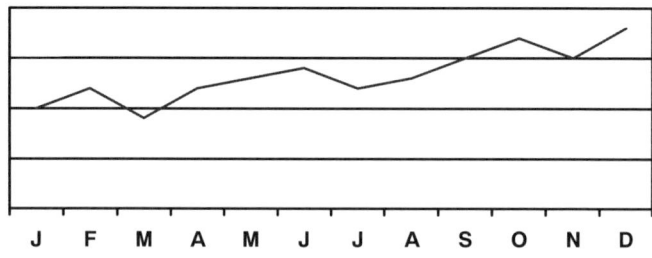

# Other Income

## Income From Miscellaneous Items

## Guideline: Dealer Specific

This K.P.I. identifies the profit or loss that you have generated from items that are not listed separately on your financial reports.

Typically, this could be Warranty Sales, Tax Disc refunds or $3^{rd}$ party accessories such as Scotchguard etc.

The total of this revenue is put into a single accounting line shown as Other or Miscellaneous.

Be careful with this one. It is a statistic that requires your investigation because it can often be used as a dumping ground for all sorts of profits or costs that have not been properly identified.

Unless you know exactly what is contained here, you could be charged for something without your knowledge or consent.

# Policy Costs

## "Certainly, we'll rectify that for you right now."

### Guideline: Own Policy

This term is also known as Policy Adjustments, Goodwill or Rectification. It refers to those costs that must be borne by the Sales Department that cannot be reclaimed or charged on to warranty or any other Department.

Just imagine that you sold a vehicle a couple of weeks ago and the customer has returned to you because there is a problem. You agree to rectify the problem for the customer, and the question is who pays the bill? If the answer is the Sales Department then this is known as a Policy Cost and is usually shown as a cost per unit sold.

Example:
(A) Policy Costs = £53,760
(B) Vehicles Sold = 960
(C) **Policy Costs per Unit** = **£56** (A ÷ B)

This K.P.I. is usually shown separately for new and used vehicles as they both deliver very different results. As you can well imagine, Policy Costs for used vehicles are generally much higher.

You can usually find your Policy Costs within the Semi-Fixed Expenses of your management accounts.

# Reconditioning Costs

## Reconditioning Costs ÷ Used Units Sold

## Guideline: Franchise Specific

This K.P.I. establishes the average amount of money that you spend on reconditioning each of your used vehicles.

Example:
(A) Reconditioning Costs         = £211,200
(B) Used Vehicles Sold           = 960
(C) **Reconditioning Costs per Unit** = **£220**  (A ÷ B)

It is very difficult to provide a benchmark for this statistic as dealer standards, specification and price of the vehicles varies considerably.

As with all K.P.I's you need to capture the trend of this statistic if you are to gain control of its direction. Keep in mind that it is only an average of your Reconditioning Costs and something such as an engine or gearbox replacement will have a significant impact on your results.

The important thing is to be aware of its trend and the reasons why it is travelling in a given direction as it is influenced by many different factors.

You can keep track of your performance by means of a simple graph that you update monthly, or at the very least, have it included within your Daily Operating Controls.

# Rectification

## "Certainly, we'll rectify that for you right now."

## Guideline: Own Policy

This term is also known as Policy Adjustments, Goodwill or Policy Costs. It refers to those costs that must be borne by the Sales Department that cannot be reclaimed or charged on to warranty or any other Department.

Just imagine that you sold a vehicle a couple of weeks ago and the customer has returned to you because there is a problem. You agree to rectify the problem for the customer, and the question is who pays the bill? If the answer is the Sales Department then this is known as Rectification and is usually shown as a cost per unit sold.

Example:
(A) Rectification = £53,760
(B) Vehicles Sold = 960
(C) **Rectification per Unit** = **£56** (A ÷ B)

This K.P.I. is usually shown separately for new and used vehicles as they both deliver very different results. As you can well imagine, Rectification for used vehicles is generally much higher. *(Not to be confused with Reconditioning Costs)*

You can usually find your Rectification within the Semi-Fixed Expenses of your management accounts.

# Retail:Trade Used Ratio

## Used Retail Units Sold ÷ Used Trade Units Sold

## Guideline: Franchise Specific

This K.P.I is specifically for used vehicles and it establishes the relationship between the number of used vehicles that you retail and the number of used vehicles that you sell to the trade.

Example:
(A) Used Retail Sales  = 960
(B) Used Trade Sales   = 640
(C) **Retail :Trade Ratio  = 1.5:1** (A ÷ B)

This example shows that for every used vehicle that you trade, you sell 1.5 retail vehicles. Take the time to understand what you are reading on your reports as some manufacturers show this ratio in reverse. (Trade: Retail)

It is not possible to provide an industry benchmark for this Key Performance Indicator as it is influenced by the franchise that you operate, your overall trading strategy and the ability of the Sales Manager.

# Return on Investment *(Used Vehicles)*

## Used Vehicle Profit ÷ Stock Value (x 100)

### Baseline: > 60%

This K.P.I measures the amount of profit that you generate from used vehicles as a percentage of the investment you have in used vehicle stock.

There are many different variations on this calculation, the example shown here is probably the most popular.

Example:
(A) Used Vehicle Gross Profit  = £480,000
(B) All Used Vehicle Expenses  = £160,000
(C) Used Vehicle Profit        = £320,000 (A - B)
(D) Used Vehicle Stock Value   = £460,000
(E) Return on Investment       = **69.56%** (C ÷ D x 100)

The logic behind this K.P.I. is straightforward in that it measures whether you are really making any profit from your used vehicle activity. Expenses that are deducted generally include Reconditioning Costs and Sales Commissions; however, some reports measure Gross Profit and do not deduct expenses, whilst others deduct further expenses such as basic salaries.

Neither method is right nor wrong; it is simply a matter of what you want to measure. However, you should invest some time in understanding what is in your own statistics because the deduction of expenses makes a sizable distortion to the final result.

# Sales Commissions

## Sales Commission ÷ Gross Profit (x 100)

## Guideline: Own Policy

This K.P.I. establishes the average amount of Sales Commission that is paid to your sales team.

Example:
(A) Sales Commissions      = £68,208
(B) Department Turnover    = £7,432,165
(C) Vehicles Sold          = 784
(D) Sales Commission p/unit = £87 (A ÷ C)
(E) **Sales Commission %** = **0.9%**  (A ÷ B x 100)

When the Sales Commissions are expressed as an average per unit or a percentage of Turnover, they are more useful to handle when comparing your performance with someone else and they can be found within the Variable Expenses of your management accounts.

The values of Sales Commission vary considerably across the country because they are dependent upon salary structures and incentive schemes. However, you will find it useful to measure the trend within your own business in order to keep them under control.

As an alternative measurement, some reports illustrate Sales Commissions as a percentage of Gross Profit as opposed to Turnover and some reports separate the amounts paid for new and used vehicles.

The provision of data separation is very useful, providing that you do something with it.

# Semi-Fixed Expenses

## Semi-Fixed Expenses ÷ Department Turnover (x 100)

## Guideline: Franchise Specific

Semi-Fixed Expenses are those expenses that are not directly linked to the number of vehicles that you sell. They represent those expenses that you have to pay to keep the department running whether you sell anything or not.

A good example here is basic salaries or advertising. If you do not sell any vehicles, you still have to pay for advertising and the basic salary for each Salesperson and the Sales Manager.

Example:
(A) Semi-Fixed Expenses      = £280,326
(B) Department Turnover      = £7,432,165
(C) Vehicles Sold            = 784
(D) Semi-Fixed Expenses p/unit = £358  (A ÷ C)
(E) **Semi-Fixed Expense %**   = **3.7%**  (A ÷ B x 100)

Typically, Semi-Fixed Expenses are shown as a monetary value per unit sold and also as a percentage of Sales Department Turnover.

The reason that they are called Semi-Fixed is that they are fixed each month irrespective of sales volume, but the Directors of the business decide at what value those expenses are fixed.

The important thing to note here is that these expenses are <u>not</u> linked to sales volume.

# Stock Turn *(Version 1)*

## Annualised Used Unit Sales ÷ Used Units in Stock

## Baseline: > 8 times per annum

Used vehicle Stock Turn tells you the number of times that you turnover your used vehicle stock in 1 year.

When considering the improvement of operational performance with used vehicles, this K.P.I. represents the kingpin around which everything else revolves.

Example:
(A) Annualised used vehicle sales = 945
(B) Number of units in used vehicle stock = 90
(C) **Annual Stock Turn = 10.5** (A ÷ B)

This example illustrates the used vehicle stock being turned 10.5 times per year. Quite simply, the faster you turn your used vehicle stock, the less money you need to invest and the more profit you will make.

Stock Turn affects your business in the two areas that really matter. Improving this K.P.I tends to increase your profitability in used vehicles and also speeds your company's Circulation of Funds Employed thereby delivering a double benefit.

If you ignore Stock Turn, then all your profits could leak out of your business just as easily as water leaking from a colander because with the passing of time, your costs become larger and your profits become smaller.

# Stock Turn *(Version 2)*

## Annual Used Sales From Stock ÷ Used Units in Stock

## Baseline: > 8 times per annum

This second version of used vehicle Stock Turn is more accurate than the first for measuring the utilisation of your used vehicle stock.

At first glance, version 1 seems to cover everything, that is until you realise that S.O.R. vehicles are not included within your used vehicle stock, but they are included within your sales!

Example:
(A) Annual used sales from stock         = 657
(B) Annual used sales from S.O.R.        = 288
(C) Annual used sales                    = 945
(D) Number of units in used vehicle stock = 90
(E) **Annual Stock Turn**                = **7.30** (A ÷ D)

The current trend of the industry is to take more S.O.R. vehicles from the manufacturer and enjoy the benefits of greater selection; smart move and long may it continue.

BUT, you cannot include the sale of these vehicles to evaluate how effective you are with the used vehicle stock that you own because you are creating a huge distortion.

To calculate your true used vehicle Stock Turn, you must only count those vehicles that have been sold from your stock. All sales from S.O.R. stock should be excluded from the equation.

# Stock Turn *(Days, Used Vehicles)*

## 365 ÷ Annual Stock Turn

## Baseline: < 45 Days

This is also known as Days Supply. The logic and thinking behind this K.P.I. is very similar to that of annual Stock Turn except that it is calculated by a slightly different method.

Example:
(A) Number of days in 1 year = 365
(B) Annual Stock Turn = 10.4
(C) **Days Stock Turn** = **35 days** (A ÷ B)

Let's say that you have 54 used vehicles in stock. The example above shows that each one of your vehicles sells every 35 days. Obviously, some of your vehicles will sell quicker than this and some will sell slower, the average being 35 days.

Now let's say that when you sell a vehicle you retain an average Gross Profit of £1,200 per unit. Armed with this information you can say that each of your 54 vehicles will produce a Gross Profit of £1,200 every 35 days.

You can now see from this example that the faster your days Stock Turn, the quicker you will get your hands on your profit and therefore less money will be absorbed in costs.

# Target Related Bonus

## Bonuses Received for Target Achievement

## Guideline: Franchise Specific

If your dealership is part of a franchise dealer network, then it is usual business practise for that franchise to set vehicle sales targets. When you achieve these targets, the franchise manufacturer pays a bonus.

The amount of bonus paid by each manufacturer varies considerably, but the thing that you should keep in mind is this. When do you show this bonus payment within your reports?

Some dealers show the bonus in the period within which it has been earned and other dealers show this bonus when they actually receive payment; the difference could be two months apart.

The variance across this method of accounting causes a sizable distortion in profitability. Some franchise manufactures are now informing their dealers to enter bonus payments at a specific time so that these distortions are eradicated and composite reports are more meaningful.

When comparing your profitability with another dealer, it is always worth establishing how and when this element of bonus is allocated.

# Used:New Retail Ratio

## Used Retail Units Sold ÷ New Retail Units Sold

## Baseline: >1:1

This K.P.I is specifically for retail vehicles and excludes all fleet sales. The statistic establishes the relationship between the number of used vehicles that you retail and the number of new vehicles that you retail.

Example:
(A) Used Retail Sales = 960
(B) New Retail Sales = 548
(C) **Used:New Retail Ratio = 1.75:1** (A ÷ B)

This example shows that for every new vehicle that you retail, you sell 1.75 used retail vehicles. Take the time to understand what you are reading on your reports as some manufacturers show this ratio in reverse. (New:Used)

It is not possible to provide an industry benchmark for this performance as it is influenced by the franchise that you operate, your overall trading strategy, the ability of the Sales Manager and the sales team.

# Used Vehicle Stock Ageing

## Stock Age Profile of Units in Stock

### Guideline: Own Policy

This information is really four Key Performance Indicators all rolled in to one. They assess your total units in stock and separate them into age categories expressed as a percentage.

Example:
(A) Units between 01 - 30 Days  = 36 - 60%
(B) Units between 31 - 60 Days  = 15 - 25%
(C) Units between 61 - 90 Days  =  6 - 10%
(D) Units over 90 Days          =  3 -  5%
(E) Total Units in Stock        = 60 - 100%

In many instances this information is shown a simple, yet very effective pie chart.

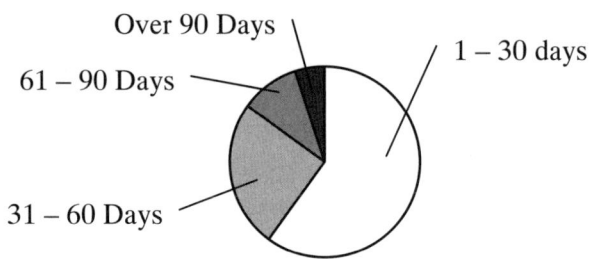

This example shows that 5% of the units that are in stock are over 90 days old. What it does not tell you is how much older than 90 days they are.

See also % Value of Stock Over 90 Days.

# Used Vehicle Stocking Plan

## Special Loan Provided For Used Vehicle Stock

## Benchmark: 80% of Stock Value

A Used Vehicle Stocking Plan is a unique type of funding where your dealership usually pays the interest on the loan and the principle loan value can vary from month to month according to the value of your used vehicle stock.

Let's say that you have an agreement to hold £250,000 of used vehicle stock at any one time. Your loan provider, usually your franchise manufacturer or their finance company, will provide you with up to 80% of that value.

Example:
(A) Agreed Stock Value    =  £250,000
(B) **Stocking Plan**     =  £200,000 (A x 80 ÷ 100)

Finance companies usually advance up to 80% of the agreed stock value because the 20% difference gives them cover for depreciation if they have to liquidate the vehicles.

An Auditor visits your dealership every month to value your stock against one of the industry guides and your stock value must exceed this figure.

If the stock valuation is above the agreed £250,000 then everything carries on as normal. However, if your stock is valued less than the agreed limit, you have to write a cheque to make up the difference of the shortfall.

# Used Vehicle Stock Value

## Value of Used Vehicle Stock at Stand In Value

### Guideline: See Stock Turn, Used Vehicles

This statistic simply provides you with the value of your used vehicle stock at any one moment in time.

The figure is usually taken directly from your Balance Sheet from which your used vehicle stock can be found within the section labelled Current Assets.

The used vehicle stock value takes into account all stock write down that has taken place within the current year and it is this figure that is used for the calculation of K.P.I's such as used vehicle Stock Turn.

It is important to note that this figure is reported as a monetary value and reflects the stand in value as opposed to the retail selling price or the original purchase price.

The information that you really want to know here is how much stock should you be holding at any one moment in time? The answers to this question lies in the K.P.I. used vehicle Stock Turn.

# Used Vehicle Write Down

## Depreciation of Used Vehicle Stock

## Guideline: Vehicle Specific

If there is one thing that is certain about used vehicles, it is that their value changes on a monthly basis and unfortunately for us, it's usually in a downward direction.

The top performing Sales Managers within our industry re-evaluate their used vehicle stock every month, and where depreciation has taken hold, the effects are shown within Used Vehicle Write Down.

Example:
(A) Current Used Stock Value = £324,500
(B) Revaluation of used stock = £320,700
(C) **Used Vehicle Write Down = £3,800**  (A - B)

The value of Used Vehicle Write Down represents the amount of depreciation that has been suffered. Typically, this value can be found within the Semi-Fixed Expenses of your management accounts.

The value of Used Vehicle Write Down is usually deducted from the stand in value of the used vehicles that have depreciated so that the screen price can be reduced.

This process serves to maintain a competitive pricing strategy for used vehicles within your marketplace without the loss of Gross Profit.

It provides you with the true trading status of your business as opposed to hiding behind lower margins.

# Variable Expenses

## Variable Expenses ÷ Departmental Turnover (x 100)

### Guideline: Own Policy

Variable Expenses are those expenses that are directly linked to the volume of business that you conduct. A good example here is Sales Commission. If you do not sell any vehicles then commission will be zero. When a Salesperson sells a vehicle, only then does the Sales Commission become payable.

Typically, Variable Expenses are shown as a monetary value and in order for you to capture meaningful trend analysis you will need to express them as a percentage of departmental Turnover.

Example:
(A) Variable Expenses      = £133,778
(B) Total Turnover         = £7,432,165
(C) **Variable Expense %** = **1.8%**   (A ÷ B x 100)

The term "Variable" does not mean that an expense varies by value, nor does it mean that it may change in some way. It simply means that this type of expense grows with the level of business that you conduct.

In order to gain full control over your Departmental Expenses you really need to understand the difference between Variable and Semi-fixed Expenses and have them properly separated on your financial reports.

# Vehicle Debtor Days

## Vehicle Debtors ÷ Vehicle Sales Daily Turnover

## Benchmark: < 14 Days

The Vehicle Debtor Days informs you of the average number of days that your customers take to pay you for their vehicles. Typically, this usually applies to Fleet Sales.

Example:
(A) Vehicle Debtors = £21,400
(B) Vehicle Sales Daily Turnover* = £3,891
(C) **Vehicle Debtor Days** = **5.5 days** (A ÷ B)

*Note:*
In order to calculate the Vehicle Sales Daily Turnover, you will need to take the total value of the vehicles sold on credit for one month and divide that figure by the number of days in that month to arrive at a daily sales turnover.

Example:*
(A) Vehicles Sold On Credit = £120,624
(B) Days in Current Month = 31
(C) Vehicle Sales Daily Turnover = £3,891   (A ÷ B)

Credit terms around the country with fleet companies vary considerably. In any event, you should ensure that you recover your money in the fastest time possible to reduce any risk and to minimise the investment.

# Interpreting Your Service Department

**Top K.P.I's to study:**

**Utilisation**
**Productivity**
**Recovery Rate**

# Typical Service Department Structure

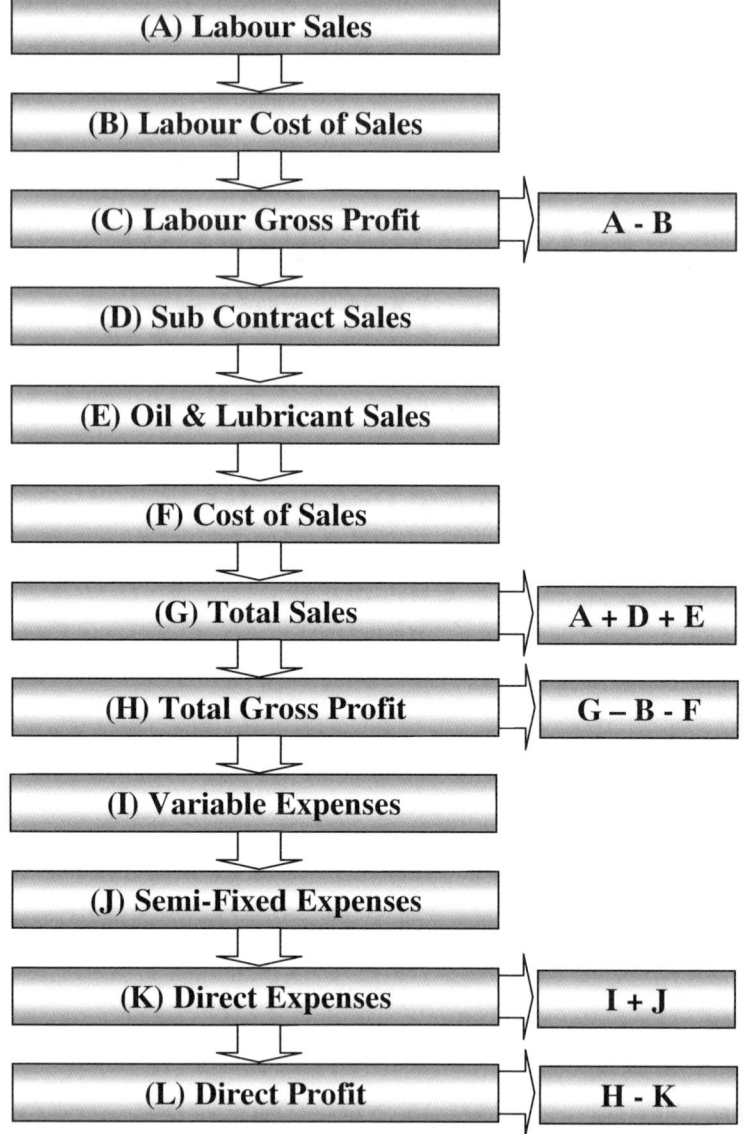

# Debtor Days

## Service Debtors ÷ Service Daily Credit Turnover

## Baseline < 45 days

The Debtor Days K.P.I is a measurement of the credit activity within the Service Department. Its purpose is to inform you of the average number of days that your customers take to pay you.

Example:
(A) Service Debtors = £80,416
(B) Service Daily Credit Turnover* = £1,870
(C) **Debtor Days** = **43 days** (A ÷ B)

*Note:*
In order to calculate the Service Daily Turnover, you will need to take the annualised Service Turnover sold on credit and divide that figure by 365 to arrive at a daily sales turnover.

Example:*
(A) Annual Turnover On Credit = £682,550
(B) Days in 1 year = 365
(C) Service Daily Credit Turnover = £1,870 (A ÷ B)

In the example provided above the average amount of debt is outstanding for a period of 43 days. In many cases, customer credit agreements are for 30 days and all too often these credit terms are not fully instigated and your money is outstanding for longer periods of time. The question is how much longer?

# Departmental Expenses

## Departmental Expenses ÷ Turnover (x100)

### Guideline: Own Policy

The Departmental Expenses of the Service Department are also know as Direct Expenses and refer to the total expenses incurred. They represent the sum total of the Variable Expenses and Semi-Fixed Expenses.

Typically, Departmental Expenses are shown as a monetary value and in order for you to capture meaningful trend analysis you will need to express them as a percentage of departmental Turnover.

Example:
(A) Variable Expenses = £18,570
(B) Semi-Fixed Expenses = £92,850
(C) **Departmental Expenses** = **£111,420** (A + B)
(D) Department Turnover = £371,388
(E) **Departmental Expense %** = **30%** (C ÷ D x 100)

Keeping control of Departmental Expenses can be a difficult task unless you fully understand the difference between Variable Expenses and Semi-Fixed Expenses.

Variable Expenses are directly linked to sales volume and Semi-Fixed Expenses are not linked to sales volume therefore the actions that you need to take to maintain control is different in each area.

# Departmental Profit %

## Departmental Profit ÷ Turnover (x100)

### Baseline: > 35%

The Departmental Profit of the Service Department is also called many other things such as, Direct Profit, Operating Profit and of course the bottom line.

You may have already deduced from the financial structure of the department at the beginning of this section that Departmental Profit is calculated by taking Gross Profit minus Departmental Expenses. To make sense of this figure it is always expressed as a percentage of Turnover when used for trending as it is the direction of travel that is of most interest to you.

Example:
(A) Departmental Profit         = £57,907
(B) Departmental Turnover       = £165,446
(C) **Departmental Profit %**   = **35%**  (A ÷ B x 100)

Keeping track of your Departmental Profit % is best shown in the form of a simple graph that is updated monthly so that you can see the trends that are emerging.

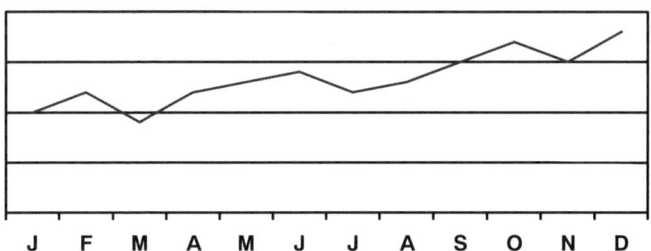

# Direct Expenses

## Direct Expenses ÷ Turnover (x100)

## Guideline: Franchise Specific

The Direct Expenses of the Service Department are also known as Departmental Expenses and refer to the total expenses incurred. They represent the sum total of the Variable Expenses and Semi-Fixed Expenses.

Typically, Direct Expenses are shown as a monetary value and in order for you to capture meaningful trend analysis you will need to express them as a percentage of departmental Turnover.

Example:
(A) Variable Expenses    = £18,570
(B) Semi-Fixed Expenses = £92,850
(C) **Direct Expenses**   = **£111,420**  (A + B)
(D) Department Turnover = £371,388
(E) **Direct Expense %**  = **30%**      (C ÷ D x 100)

Keeping control of Direct Expenses can be a difficult task unless you fully understand the difference between Variable Expenses and Semi-Fixed Expenses.

Variable Expenses are directly linked to sales volume and Semi-Fixed Expenses are not linked to sales volume therefore the actions that you need to take to maintain control is different in each area.

# Direct Profit %

## Direct Profit ÷ Turnover (x100)

### Baseline: > 35%

The Direct Profit of the Service Department is also called many other things such as, Departmental Profit, Operating Profit and of course the bottom line.

Direct Profit is calculated by taking Gross Profit minus Departmental Expenses. To make sense of this figure it is always expressed as a percentage of Turnover when used for trending as it is the direction of travel that is of most interest to you.

Example:
(A) Direct Profit = £57,907
(B) Departmental Turnover = £165,446
(C) **Direct Profit %** = **35%** (A ÷ B x 100)

Keeping track of your Direct Profit % is best shown in the form of a simple graph that is updated monthly so that you can see the trends that are emerging.

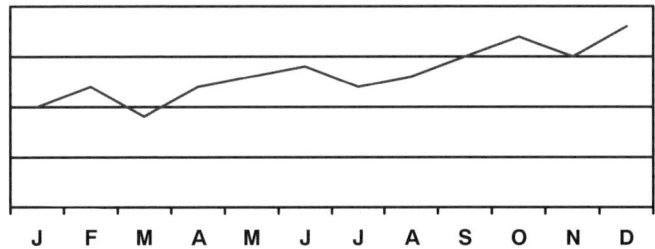

# Diverted Time

## Hours Attended – Hours Worked

## Guideline: See Utilisation

This term is also known as Unrecovered Time, Idle Time or Lost Time.

Diverted Time means that the Technicians have been diverted onto tasks that cannot be charged out to the customer. Typically this could be time spent locating a vehicle, waiting for parts and other such issues.

Example:
(A) Hours Attended = 320
(B) Hours Worked = 304
(C) **Hours Diverted** = **16** (A - B)
(D) Prime labour Cost = £8.50
(E) **Diverted Time** = **£136** (C x D)

The mathematical formula is simply Hours Attended minus Hours Worked and this is always shown as a monetary value, which can usually be found within the Variable Expenses of the Service Department.

In addition to this some financial reports might show the monetary value of Diverted Time as a percentage of the Departmental Gross Profit.

(Also see Hours Attended and Hours Worked)

# Gross Profit %

## Gross Profit ÷ Turnover (x100)

## Baseline: > 65%

Within the Service Department there are two levels of Gross Profit that are measured; be sure that you are measuring the results that you really want.

The basic concept of Gross Profit is simply sale less cost of sale, therefore the following example relates to the Service Department as a whole.

Example:
(A) Total Gross Profit = £107,540
(B) Turnover = £165,446
(C) **Gross Profit %** = **65%**   (A ÷ B x 100)

The trading strategy of your Service Department will have an impact upon the suggested baseline of 65% and will vary according to the level of discount that you give, Sub Contract work and oil sales that your business conducts.

Financial reports for the Service Department show Labour Gross Profit before they show the total Departmental Gross Profit; this page is explaining the overall Departmental Gross Profit within which Labour Gross Profit is included.

*(Also see Labour Gross Profit.)*

# Hours Attended

## Total Number of Productive Hours Available

### Guideline: See Hours Bought

This term represents the total number of hours that the Technicians are available to work, or in other words, the total number of hours that the Technicians are clocked-in at the dealership.

The number of Hours Attended is the statistic that is used in the calculation of Utilisation and Overall Efficiency.

It is important to note that this does not give you the total number of Hours Worked; it provides you with the total number of hours that are *available* to work.

As well as collating the total number of Hours Attended, it is also recommended that you calculate the hours attended for each individual Technician so that their individual Utilisation can be ascertained.

Factors that will influence the number of Hours Attended is time spent on training courses, time off on holiday, and sickness.

*(Also see Hours Bought)*

# Hours Bought

## Total Number of Hours Paid to Technicians

## Guideline: See Hours Attended

This term represents the total number of hours that you pay your Technicians, or in other words it represents the total Technicians salary for the specified period.

It includes time spent at the dealership, time spent on training courses, sickness and holiday pay.

Example:
| | | |
|---|---|---|
| (A) Training | = 80 hours | (2 weeks) |
| (B) Holiday | = 160 Hours | (4 weeks) |
| (C) Sickness | = 40 hours | (1 week) |
| (D) Attended Hours | = 1800 | (45 weeks) |
| **(E) Total Hours Bought** | **= 2080** | (52 weeks) |

For statistical purposes, and the calculation of key performance indicators, Hours Bought is never considered in any equation. For the most part, it is usually seen in business plans and annual budgets so that an accurate forecast of costs can be attained.

For instance, there are fifty-two weeks in the year of which four weeks could be allocated to holiday, two weeks allocated to training, and one week could be allocated for sickness.

Simply by multiplying the hourly rate that you pay to your Technicians you are able to calculate a reasonably accurate forecast in each sector listed.

# Hours per Parc

## Annualised Hours Sold ÷ Number of Vehicles in Parc

## Guideline: Own Strategy

This K.P.I. is very useful for assessing your current performance in Hours Sold against your fellow dealers or your total market potential.

Example:
(A) Annual hours sold  = 22,752
(B) Number of vehicles in parc  = 7,584
(C) **Hours sold per parc vehicle** = 3  (A ÷ B)

Keep in mind that this statistic is utilising every vehicle in the parc and if you are assessing a 10-year parc some of those vehicles may no longer be in your area or even in existence.

You may also wish to consider who else is registering vehicles within your territory it could be that you have a sizeable fleet that is distorting your vehicle parc. You also have to ask yourself the question about the age profile of the vehicles that your dealership attracts.

Many financial reports show the statistic averaged over the whole vehicle parc, however your franchise manufacturer should be able to provide you with your parc data on a year-by-year basis, and in some cases on a model-by-model basis too. This will provide you with a more realistic and accurate figure with which to measure your territory penetration.

# Hours per Retail Job Card

## Retail Hours Sold ÷ Number of Retail Job Cards

### Guideline: > 2 hrs

This K.P.I. simply counts the number of retail hours that have been sold and the number of job cards that have been raised in the retail sector and one is simply divided by the other to give an average number of hours sold per retail job.

Example:
(A) Number of Retail Hours Sold = 1,437
(B) Number of Retail Job Cards = 334
(C) **Hours per Retail Job Card** = **4.3**  (A ÷ B)

When you wish to compare your performance with another dealer it is often difficult to gain an accurate measurement by using Labour Sales or the number of Hours Sold, as no two dealers are the same; this is where manufacturers composites and inter-firm comparisons are very useful.

When you compare your results to the national average you should keep in mind that this statistic is influenced by the type of work that is being undertaken, the Technicians ability to find additional work and the Service Receptionist's ability to sell that additional requirement on to the customer.

# Hours Sold

### Total Number of Hours Invoiced

### Guideline: See Labour Sales Mix

This figure represents the total number of hours that have been invoiced. Of course, the monetary value of this statistic is represented by the Labour Sales value.

It is more important to keep track of the number of Hours Sold than it is to keep track of their monetary value. This is because the monetary value of the Hours Sold can be influenced by your charge out rate and Recovery Rate and this does not therefore provide you with an accurate reflection of the direction of your business.

By far the easiest way to track the performance of the Hours Sold is to compile them into a simple graph on a weekly or monthly basis.

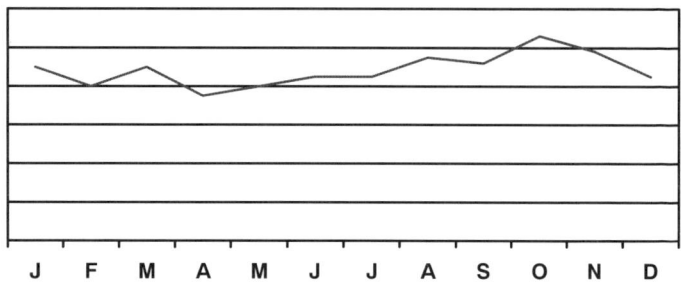

The graph will of course be more meaningful if you are able to segregate the hours sold between Retail, Internal and Warranty so that you can accurately plot the trend in each performance sector.

# Hours Worked

## Hours Attended – Idle Time

## Guideline: See Utilisation

This statistic represents the number of hours that the Technicians have been working productively.

Working productively means, spanner-in-hand head-under-bonnet working on time that can be charged out to the customer. Although a Technician may be clocked in and available to work for 40 hours per week, the time that they spent working productively is shown as the Hours Worked.

Example:
(A) Hours Attended = 40
(B) Idle Time = 2
(C) **Hours Worked = 38** (A - B)

There is only one way to accurately capture the number of Hours Worked productively and that is for each Technician to clock on and off each individual job.

Whatever your thoughts in this area of analysis there is one question that must be asked. If you do not accurately record this key performance area, when you do have a problem that you want to resolve, where do you begin to look for the answers? There is an old quote that says:
"If you can't measure it, you can't manage it."

# Idle Time

## Hours Attended – Hours Worked

## Guideline: See Utilisation

Idle Time does not mean that the Technicians are standing around idle doing nothing; it simply represents the time spent at the dealership that cannot be charged out to the customer. This is also known as Diverted Time, Unrecovered Time or Lost Time.

Typically this could be time spent locating keys or vehicles, waiting for parts and other such issues.

Example:
| | | |
|---|---|---|
| (A) Hours Attended | = 320 | |
| (B) Hours Worked | = 304 | |
| (C) **Hours Idle** | = **16** | (A - B) |
| (D) Prime labour Cost | = £8.50 | |
| (E) **Idle Time** | = **£136** | (C x D) |

The mathematical formula is simply Hours Attended minus Hours Worked and this is always shown as a monetary value, which can usually be found within the Variable Expenses of the Service Department.

In addition to this, some financial reports might show the monetary value of Idle Time as a percentage of the Departmental Gross Profit.

(Also see Hours Attended and Hours Worked)

# Labour Cost of Sales

## Value of Hours Attended - Idle Time

## Baseline: 90% of Attended Hours

This statistic captures the amount of money that is paid to Technicians for every hour that is worked productively.

The amount of money that you pay your Technicians per hour is divided into three sections: Hours Attended, Hours Worked Productively and Idle Time.

Hours Attended simply represents the number of hours that the Technicians have been clocked in and available to work, these hours are simply divided between Hours Worked Productively and Idle Time.

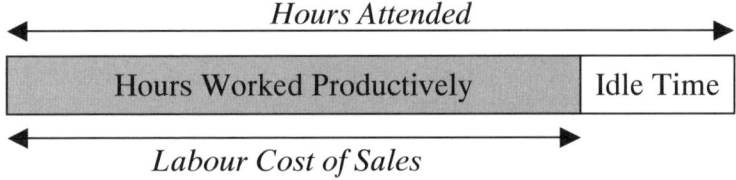

This example demonstrates that the cost of labour for the hours that have been sold can only be the hours spent working productively, and therefore Idle Time is shown as a Variable Expense.

Example:
(A) Value of Hours Attended  = £6,290
(B) Idle Time  = £320
(C) **Labour Cost of Sales**  = **£5,970**  (A - B)

# Labour Efficiency %

## Hours Worked ÷ Hours Attended (x100)

### Benchmark: 85% to 95%

This K.P.I is also known as Utilisation, Labour Utilisation and Selling Efficiency. The statistic tells you how much of the Technicians Attended time is actually spent working productively.

In more simplistic terms, each Technician usually clocks in and is available for eight hours each day, but how much of that time is spent spanner-in-hand, head-under-bonnet, working on hours that can be charged out to the customer? Labour Efficiency gives you the answer to this question.

Example:
(A) Hours Worked = 957
(B) Hours Attended = 1,040
(C) **Labour Efficiency** = **92%** (A ÷ B x 100)

This example shows that the Technicians have attended 1,040 hours at the dealership of which 92% of that time has been spent working productively. The remaining 8% will be shown in your expenses as Idle Time.

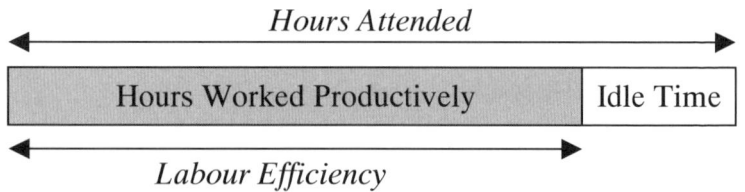

# Labour Gross Profit

## Labour Sales - Labour Cost of Sales

## Guideline: See Labour Gross Profit %

This is probably one of the most misunderstood calculations of all and is therefore worthy of your full consideration.

Most people are of the assumption that the Labour Gross Profit is Labour Sales minus Hours Attended. If this were to be the case then Idle Time would be reported at zero.

The true calculation is the monetary value of the Hours Sold minus the monetary value of the Hours Worked productively.

Example:
(A) Labour Sales *(hours sold)* = £42,240
(B) Hours Worked Productively = £7,803
(C) **Labour Gross Profit** = **£34,437** (A – B)

It is important to note here that the Labour Cost of Sales is only the value of the hours spent working productively on the hours that have been sold. You can deduce from this calculation that the Technicians time is split between hours worked productively and Idle Time.

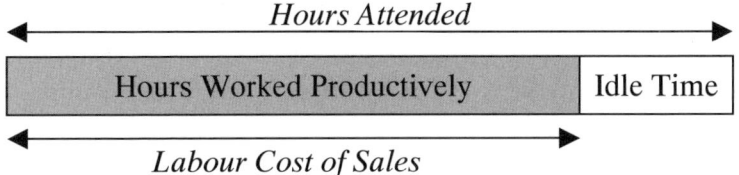

# Labour Gross Profit %

## Labour Gross Profit ÷ Labour Sales (x 100)

### Baseline: >75%

Before you read this page, please read Labour Gross Profit to ensure that you have the true understanding of the performance area that your are measuring.

This K.P.I. tells you the percentage of money you have retained from the Hours Sold after you have paid your Technicians.

Example:
(A) Labour Gross Profit = £34,437
(B) Labour Sales = £42,240
(C) **Labour Gross Profit** = **81.53%** (A ÷ B x 100)

All profit-related K.P.I's are usually measured against turnover, and in this instance the starting figure for your profit retention in the Service Department is 75%.

You could also view this to mean that you pay your Technicians less than 25% of the value of the Hours Sold for the hours that they have worked productively.

It is important to maintain a high profit margin in this K.P.I. because the Departmental Expenses erode much of it away. Therefore if your performance in this area is below 75%, you will struggle to achieve a reasonable level of profitability when you reach the Direct Profit of your department.

# Labour Sales Mix

## (Sector) Hours Sold ÷ Total Hours Sold (x100)

### Guideline: See Hours Sold

This information simply informs you of the balance between your Service Department's sales of hours.

In most cases the Service Department is split into three distinct categories of income, which are Retail, Internal, and Warranty. For many franchises it is generally accepted that the Labour Sales Mix is:

| | |
|---|---|
| Retail hours sold | 70% |
| Warranty hours sold | 10% |
| Internal hours sold | 20% |
| Total Hours sold | 100% |

It is always wise to measure your Labour Sales Mix in terms Hours Sold as opposed to the monetary value of Labour Sales because Recovery Rates vary across each income sector as do the charge out rates.

All of these price differences lead to inconsistency when measuring the trend and direction of your Service Department and it is therefore more meaningful to measure the Hours Sold into each income sector.

All of the price differences and distortions are eradicated when only the Hours Sold are analysed.

(Also see Retail:Internal ratio)

# Labour Utilisation %

### Hours Worked ÷ Hours Attended (x100)

### Benchmark: 85% to 95%

This K.P.I is also known as Utilisation, Labour Efficiency and Selling Efficiency. The statistic tells you how much of the Technicians attended time is actually spent working productively.

In more simplistic terms, each Technician usually clocks in and is available for eight hours each day, but how much of that time is spent spanner-in-hand, head-under-bonnet, working on hours that can be charged out to the customer? Labour Utilisation gives you the answer to this question.

Example:
(A) Hours Worked        = 957
(B) Hours Attended      = 1,040
(C) **Labour Utilisation**  = **92%**   (A ÷ B x 100)

This example shows that the Technicians have Attended 1,040 hours at the dealership of which 92% of that time has been spent working productively. The remaining 8% will be shown in your expenses as Idle Time.

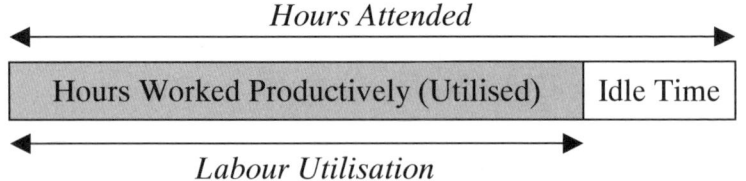

# Lead Time

## "I want my vehicle serviced, when can you fit it in?"

### Benchmark: 3 days or less

The Lead Time is the length of time a customer must wait before their vehicle can be seen by your Service Department.

A short Lead Time of two to three days is usually expected and generally accepted by a customer unless they have a serious problem that needs immediate attention.

A long Lead Time of seven to ten days is not generally understood or accepted by customer and usually results in them taking their vehicles elsewhere.

Factors that affect the length of Lead Time are Utilisation, customer retention, and Aftersales marketing. The length of Lead Time that your dealership has is really a reflection of the work that is available to you and your ability to cope with its demand.

If your Lead Time is seven days or more on a consistent basis, then you should certainly examine your Utilisation, and you may consider taking on an additional Technician if you have the facilities available.

If your Lead Time is nonexistent on a continual basis, then your Aftersales marketing campaigns may need an extra boost to gain additional work.

# Lost Time

## Hours Attended – Hours Worked

## Guideline: See Utilisation

This term is also known as Unrecovered Time, Idle Time and Diverted Time.

Lost Time means that the Technicians have been diverted onto tasks that cannot be charged out to the customer and as such the chargeable time is therefore lost. Typically this could be time spent locating a vehicle, waiting for parts and other such issues.

Example:
| | | |
|---|---|---|
| (A) Hours Attended | = 320 | |
| (B) Hours Worked | = 304 | |
| (C) **Hours Lost** | = **16** | (A - B) |
| (D) Prime labour Cost | = £8.50 | |
| (E) **Lost Time** | = **£136** | (C x D) |

The mathematical formula is simply Hours Attended minus Hours Worked and this is always shown as a monetary value, which can usually be found within the Variable Expenses of the Service Department.

In addition to this some financial reports might show the monetary value of Lost Time as a percentage of the Departmental Gross Profit.

(Also see Hours Attended and Hours Worked)

# Oil & Lubricants Profitability

## Oil Gross Profit ÷ Oil Sales (x 100)

### Baseline: > 50%

As an industry, we take a high profit margin from the sale of oil and lubricants. There is always a debate to be had as to whether the sale of oil and lubricants should be shown within the Service Department or the Parts Department. Most manufacturers financial reports show this statistic within the Service Department, which provides the reason for it being shown in this section of the book, however your financial reports may show it in the Parts Department.

Example:
(A) Oil Sales           = £10,357
(B) Oil Cost of Sales   = £3,936
(C) Oil Gross Profit    = £6,421   (A – B)
(C) **Gross Profit on Oil Sales** = **62%**   (C ÷ A x 100)

Most financial reports include the value of oil sales together with the value of oil gross profit; however, it is more meaningful to show the percentage of gross profit that has been retained for trend analysis.

*Special note:*
*In order to measure this information accurately, you need to capture the opening oil stock and the closing oil stock at the end of each period, taking into account any oil purchases and from this you can determine how much oil has been used. This of course is your true cost of sale. If you do not currently use this method, and your oil is not metered, how do you account for your oil?*

# Operating Profit %

## Operating Profit ÷ Turnover (x100)

### Baseline: > 35%

The Operating Profit of the Service Department is also called many other things such as, Direct Profit, and of course the bottom line.

Operating Profit is exactly the same as Departmental Profit and is calculated by taking Gross Profit minus Departmental Expenses. To make sense of this figure it is always expressed as a percentage of Turnover when used for trending as it is the direction of travel that is of most interest.

Example:
(A) Operating Profit      = £57,907
(B) Departmental Turnover = £165,446
(C) **Operating Profit %** = **35%**  (A ÷ B x 100)

Keeping track of your Operating Profit % is best shown in the form of a simple graph that is updated monthly so that you can see the trends that are emerging.

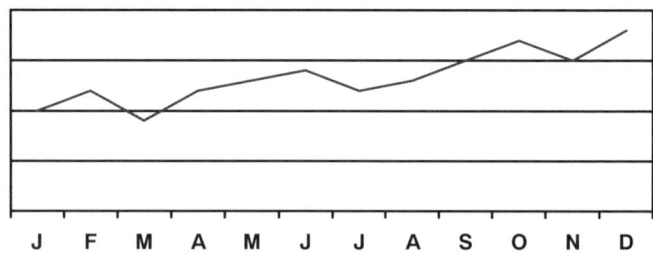

# Overall Efficiency %

## Hours Sold ÷ Hours Attended (x100)

## Benchmark: 95% to 115%

This K.P.I measures the relationship between the number of hours that have been sold and the number of hours that the Technicians have been available to work.

Example:
(A) Hours Sold = 1,130
(B) Hours Attended = 1,040
(C) **Overall Efficiency** = **108%**   (A ÷ B x 100)

This example shows that the Service Department has successfully sold more hours than the Technicians have Attended, therefore the Overall Efficiency of the department is in excess of 100%.

The direction and travel of this key performance indicator keeps you informed of the balance and harmony that must exist between your Utilisation and Productivity.

Overall Efficiency clearly demonstrates that there is little point in increasing one and ignoring the other.

Example:
(A) Utilisation = 92%
(B) Productivity = 118%
(C) **Overall Efficiency** = **108.56%**   (A x B ÷ 100)

# Parts Sales per Labour Hour

## Parts Sales to the Workshop ÷ Hours Sold

## Guideline: Generally equal to labour rate

This K.P.I. produces a monetary figure that is the average value of parts sold for every labour hour that is sold. It is a statistic that informs you whether your Technicians are *repairing* or *replacing* parts.

Example:
(A) Parts Sales to the Workshop = £42,240
(B) Hours Sold = 870
(C) **Parts Sales per Labour Hour = £48.55**  (A ÷ B)

Hypothetically, let's say that the national average for this K.P.I is £30. The example above might suggest that your Technicians are finding additional work when vehicles come into the workshop and parts are being replaced as opposed to being repaired.

On the other hand if the national average is reported at £65 the example above might suggest that your Technicians are failing to find additional work and parts are being repaired as opposed to being replaced.

Of course there are many factors that influence this statistic, not least of which being the type and mix of work that you are undertaking.

In order to gain meaningful statistics this K.P.I. must be calculated separately for Retail, Internal and Warranty.

# Policy Costs

**"Certainly, we'll rectify that as a gesture of goodwill."**

**Guideline: Own Policy**

This term is also known as Policy Adjustments, Goodwill or Rectification. It refers to those costs that must be borne by the Service Department that cannot be reclaimed or charged on to warranty or any other Department.

Let's say that three days ago you fitted a new exhaust system for one of your customers, and now they are back in front of you with a problem. They are saying that the exhaust system is rattling and of course they are not happy.

Naturally, you cannot expect the customer to pay any more money, as they have only just paid you to have the exhaust system fitted. Therefore you agree to rectify the problem for the customer, and the question is who pays the bill?

Since this job is the direct responsibility of the Service Department, it cannot be charged onto warranty or any other department and therefore the hours spent on the rectification is accounted for within Policy Costs in your management accounts.

# Productive Efficiency %

## Hours Sold ÷ Hours Worked Productively (x100)

### Benchmark: 110% to 125%

This K.P.I. is also known as Productivity and Working Efficiency. It shows you your Technicians ability to complete their work within the franchise manufacturers allocated time schedules.

Example:
(A) Hours Sold = 1,130
(B) Hours Worked productively = 957
(C) **Productive Efficiency** = **118%** (A ÷ B x 100)

Most franchise manufacturers provide dealers with allocated times for jobs on all vehicles and this allocated time is the maximum amount that you are able to charge your customer.

In order to make gains in profitability, your Technicians must complete the job in a lesser time than is allocated by the manufacturer, thereby increasing your Productive Efficiency.

Productive Efficiency is a double-edged sword. If your Technicians take more time to complete the job than the manufacturers allocated time then your profitability diminishes and Productive Efficiency falls below 100%.

# Productive Ratio

## Productive staff ÷ Non-Productive staff

## Guideline: 3:1

This K.P.I. measures the ratio between productive staff and non-productive staff.

Typically, non-productive staff could be the Service Manager, Service Receptionist and Warranty Clerk

Example:
(A) Productive staff = 12
(B) Non-Productive staff = 4
(C) **Productive Ratio** = **3:1** (A ÷ B)

Composite results appear to average at around 3:1, or in other words, for every 3 Technicians that you employ, you have 1 member of staff who is non-productive.

This ratio can vary wildly and is dependant upon how you apportion your Apprentices and Foreman. Obviously, if your Productive Ratio is lower than 3:1 you will need to take corrective action.

Make sure that you understand what you are looking at when you read this information as some financial reports show this equation in reverse.

# Productivity %

**Hours Sold ÷ Hours Worked Productively (x100)**

**Benchmark: 110% to 125%**

This K.P.I. is also known as Productive Efficiency or Working Efficiency. It shows you your Technicians ability to complete their work within the franchise manufacturers allocated time schedules.

Example:
(A) Hours Sold = 1,130
(B) Hours Worked productively = 957
(C) **Productivity** = **118%** (A ÷ B x 100)

Most franchise manufacturers provide dealers with allocated times for jobs on all vehicles and this allocated time is the maximum amount that you are able to charge your customer.

In order to make gains in profitability, your Technicians must complete the job in a lesser time than is allocated by the manufacturer, thereby increasing your Productivity.

Productivity is a double-edged sword. If your Technicians take more time to complete the job than the manufacturers allocated time then your profitability diminishes and Productivity falls below 100%.

# Productive Staff : Non-Productive Staff

## Productive staff ÷ Non-Productive staff

## Guideline: 3:1

This K.P.I. measures the ratio between productive staff and non-productive staff and is sometimes called the Productive Ratio.

Typically, non-productive staff could be the Service Manager, Service Receptionist and Warranty Clerk

Example:
(A) Productive staff = 12
(B) Non-Productive staff = 4
(C) **Productive : Non Productive = 3:1** (A ÷ B)

Composite results appear to average at around 3:1, or in other words, for every 3 Technicians that you employ, you have 1 member of staff who is non-productive.

This statistic can vary wildly and is dependent upon how you apportion your Apprentices and Foreman. Obviously, if your Productive/Non Productive K.P.I. is lower than 3:1 you will need to take corrective action.

Make sure that you understand what you are looking at when you read this information as some financial reports show this equation in reverse.

# Recovery Rate

## Labour Sales ÷ Hours Sold

## Baseline: 95% of Charge out Rate

Your Service Department will have a published labour rate per hour, but how often are you able to charge this amount to every customer on every job?

Recovery Rate tells you how much revenue you have <u>actually</u> recovered per Hour Sold as opposed to how much you would have generated should you have applied your full charge out rate.

Example:
(A) Labour Sales = £42,240
(B) Hours Sold = 870
(C) **Recovery Rate** = **£48.55** (A ÷ B)

If we say that the published labour rate for the above example is £50 per hour, then if no discount were to be given the Labour Sales would have been £43,500.

The reality of the situation confirms that you are often forced to provide a discount in some instances, which of course reduces the amount of revenue that you are able to collect. The question is how much money have you managed to recover?

The key to success with this K.P.I is to capture individual Recovery Rates for each income sector (See Labour Sales Mix) so that you can accurately pinpoint the areas in which discount is being given.

# Rectification

**"Certainly, we'll rectify that as a gesture of goodwill."**

## Guideline: Own Policy

This term is also known as Policy Adjustments or Goodwill. It refers to those costs that must be borne by the Service Department that cannot be reclaimed or charged on to warranty or any other Department.

Let's say that three days ago you fitted a new exhaust system for one of your customers, and now they are back in front of you with a problem. They are saying that the exhaust system is rattling and of course they are not happy.

Naturally, you cannot expect the customer to pay any more money, as they have only just paid you to have the exhaust system fitted. Therefore you agree to rectify the problem for the customer, and the question is who pays the bill?

Since this job is the direct responsibility of the Service Department, it cannot be charged onto warranty or any other department and therefore the hours spent putting the right is accounted for within Rectification in your management accounts.

# Repair Orders per Technician

## Number of Repair Orders ÷ Number of Technicians

### Guideline: Own Policy

This is another of those key performance indicators that is used to level the playing field when comparing one dealer with another dealer.

It removes the emotion of the big numbers that may be involved and produces an average number of jobs that an individual Technician undertakes in a given period.

Example:
(A) Total Repair Orders = 1,458
(B) Number of Technicians = 6
(C) **Repair Orders per Technician = 243**  (A ÷ B)

There are a multitude of factors will affect this statistic including Productivity, Utilisation, and the type of work being undertaken and of course the Technicians skill.

This K.P.I is probably more useful in the preparation of budgets and business plans as opposed to measuring the effectiveness of your Technicians.

# Retail : Internal Ratio

## Retail Hours Sold ÷ Internal Hours Sold

## Baseline: 2:1

At the time of writing this book, this K.P.I is not evident in any manufacturers composites or financial reports. It provides you with the rate and direction of growth of the Service Department by understanding the relationship between the sale of retail hours and internal hours.

Example:
(A) Retail Hours Sold = 870
(B) Internal Hours Sold = 378
(C) **Retail : Internal Ratio** = **2.3:1** (A ÷ B)

One of the factors that will affect this statistic is as a rapid growth rate in vehicle sales, which in the short-term will shift the bias to internal work. However in the following months the balance should be redressed as these vehicles return for scheduled servicing.

If the underlying trend of this K.P.I is demonstrating a high dependence upon internal work, it could mean that your dealership is losing its retail customers, there are no efforts in place to grow the retail sector of your business, or there is little or no control for invoicing procedures between the Sales and Service Department.

When you wish to measure the true growth rate and direction of your Service Department then this is the K.P.I to put in place.

# Revenue per Technician

## Department Turnover ÷ Number of Technicians

## Guideline: Own Policy

This is another of those key performance indicators that is used to level the playing field when comparing one dealer with another dealer.

It removes the emotion of the big numbers that may be involved and produces an average monetary value of Turnover per Technician in any given period.

Example:
(A) Service Department Turnover = £55,404
(B) Number of Technicians = 6
(C) **Revenue per Technician** = **£9,234** (A ÷ B)

This K.P.I is probably more useful in the preparation of budgets and business plans as opposed to measuring the effectiveness of your Technicians.

*Special Note:*
There is a variation across reports with this calculation so be sure that you are measuring the correct statistics. Some reports class the revenue as Total Department Turnover, whilst others class revenue as the total value of the Hours Sold.

Neither of these statistics is either right or wrong, but do take the time to find out what is included or excluded from your own information.

# Selling Efficiency %

## Hours Worked ÷ Hours Attended (x100)

### Benchmark: 85% to 95%

This K.P.I is also known as Utilisation, Labour Efficiency and Labour Utilisation. The statistic tells you how much of the Technicians Attended time is actually spent working productively.

In more simplistic terms, each Technician usually clocks in and is available for eight hours each day, but how much of that time is spent spanner-in-hand, head-under-bonnet, working on hours that can be charged out to the customer? Selling Efficiency gives you the answer to this question.

Example:
(A) Hours Worked       = 957
(B) Hours Attended     = 1,040
(C) **Selling Efficiency** = **92%**   (A ÷ B x 100)

This example shows that the Technicians have Attended 1,040 hours at the dealership of which 92% of that time has been spent working productively. The remaining 8% will be shown in your expenses as Idle Time.

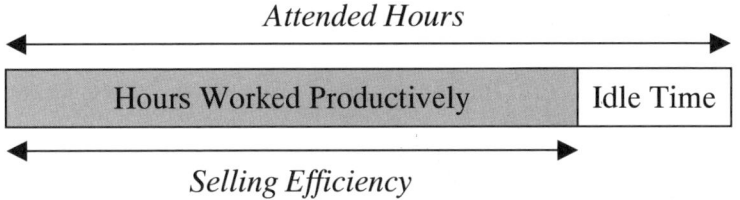

# Semi-Fixed Expenses

## Semi-Fixed Expenses ÷ Total Turnover (x 100)

### Guideline: Own Policy

Semi-Fixed Expenses are those expenses that are not directly linked to the volume of business that you conduct.

They represent those expenses that you have to pay to keep the department running whether you sell anything or not.

A good example here is non-productive salaries. If you do not sell anything, you still have to pay the Service Receptionist and Service Manager.

Example:
(A) Semi-Fixed Expenses   = £92,850
(B) Total Turnover         = £371,388
(C) **Semi-Fixed Expense % = 25%**   (A ÷ B x 100)

Typically, Semi-Fixed Expenses are shown as a monetary value and in order for you to capture meaningful trend analysis you will need to express them as a percentage of departmental Turnover.

The reason that they are called Semi-Fixed is that they are fixed each month irrespective of sales volume, but the Directors of the business decide at what value those expenses are fixed.

The important thing to note here is that these expenses are not linked to sales volume.

# Service Sales per Parc Unit

## Annualised Labour Sales ÷ Vehicles in Parc

## Guideline: Own Policy

This is a key performance indicator that you need to thoroughly examine and fully understand before you make any judgements whatsoever as it makes some far-reaching assumptions. Its purpose it to ascertain the value of Service Sales that you are achieving across your vehicle parc.

Example:
(A) Annualised Labour Sales     = £664,848
(B) Vehicle Parc                = 1,560
(C) **Service Sales Per Parc Unit** = **£426**  (A ÷ B)

Different manufacturers account for Vehicle Parc over different spans of time. For instance, some manufacturers use a five-year parc, some use a seven-year parc and others use ten years.

Also note that the age span of vehicle parc for the Service Department is often different to that of the Parts Department. Be sure to obtain the correct interpretation from your respective manufacturer.

The example above shows that for every vehicle in the parc there is an average spend of £426. However, a far more useful and accurate method of calculating territory penetration is to measure Vehicle Parc on a year-by-year basis. Please see Vehicle Parc for a more detailed explanation.

# Sub Contract Profitability

## Sub Contract GP ÷ Sub Contract Sales (x 100)

### Baseline: > 15%

Sub Contract refers to the jobs that you take in and undertake a 3rd party to conduct on your behalf. An example of this might be the fitting of windscreens for instance.

Example:
(A) Sub contract Gross Profit = £784
(B) Sub contract Sales = £5,223
(C) **Gross Profit on Oil Sales** = **15%**  (A ÷ B x 100)

Profitability in this area of the business varies greatly between manufacturers. For some truck manufacturers it can be as low as 5% and for some car manufacturers it can be as high as 25%.

There are many reasons for this high tolerance in performance and one of the main reasons being breakdown and recovery.

There are some dealers that do not make any profit margin from Sub Contract sales and research confirms that fear is the key to this shortfall. In other words, the Service Receptionist simply does not add any profit margin to the invoice when recharging the work on to the customer.

This is a thoughtful yet dangerous action to take after all, your dealership is still liable for the work that has been carried out!

# Utilisation %

## Hours Worked ÷ Hours Attended (x100)

## Benchmark: 85% to 95%

This K.P.I is also known as Labour Efficiency, Labour Utilisation and Selling Efficiency. The statistic tells you how much of the Technicians Attended time is actually spent working productively.

In more simplistic terms, each Technician usually clocks in and is available for eight hours each day, but how much of that time is spent spanner-in-hand, head-under-bonnet, working on hours that can be charged out to the customer? Utilisation gives you the answer to this question.

Example:
(A) Hours Worked = 957
(B) Hours Attended = 1,040
(C) **Utilisation** = **92%** (A ÷ B x 100)

This example shows that the Technicians have attended 1,040 hours at the dealership of which 92% of that time has been spent working productively. The remaining 8% will be shown in your expenses as Idle Time.

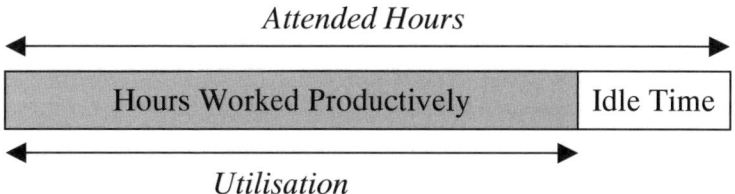

# Variable Expenses

## Variable Expenses ÷ Total Turnover (x 100)

### Guideline: Own Policy

Variable Expenses are those expenses that are directly linked to the volume of business that you conduct. A good example here is consumables. If you do not sell any hours then consumables will be zero, as soon as you begin to sell hours then consumables build accordingly.

Typically, Variable Expenses are shown as a monetary value and in order for you to capture meaningful trend analysis you will need to express them as a percentage of departmental Turnover.

Example:
(A) Variable Expenses = £18,570
(B) Total Turnover = £371,388
(C) **Variable Expense %** = **5%** (A ÷ B x 100)

The term "Variable" does not mean that an expense varies by value, nor does it mean that it may change in some way. It simply means that this type of expense grows with the level of business that you conduct.

In order to gain full control over your Departmental Expenses you really need to understand the difference between Variable and Semi-Fixed Expenses and have them separated on your financial reports.

# Vehicle Parc

Your franchise manufacturer provides you with all the vehicles registered within your dealership's area of responsibility over a given period of time; this represents your vehicle parc. These vehicles could be registered by your dealership or by another dealership that is selling vehicles into your area. In many cases the time period for measuring vehicle parc spans 10 years, although this varies from manufacturer to manufacturer.

Example:
Vehicles registered in current year = 958
Vehicles registered in Year 2 = 821
Vehicles registered in Year 3 = 767
Vehicles registered in Year 4 = 789
Vehicles registered in Year 5 = 745
Vehicles registered in Year 6 = 827
Vehicles registered in Year 7 = 754
Vehicles registered in Year 8 = 706
Vehicles registered in Year 9 = 635
Vehicles registered in Year 10 = 582
Total 10-year vehicle parc = 7,584

In the years that follow, the current vehicle registrations are added and year 10 of the calculation and is replaced with the year 9 statistics and so on, therefore providing a revised ten-year vehicle parc.

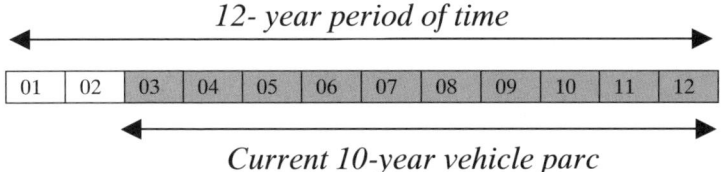

# Working Efficiency %

## Hours Sold ÷ Hours Worked Productively (x100)

### Benchmark: 110% to 125%

This K.P.I. is also known as Productivity and Productive Efficiency. It shows you your Technicians ability to complete their work within the franchise manufacturers allocated time schedules.

Example:
(A) Hours Sold = 1,130
(B) Hours Worked productively = 957
(C) **Working Efficiency** = **118%**  (A ÷ B x 100)

Most franchise manufacturers provide dealers with allocated times for jobs on all vehicles and this allocated time is the maximum amount that you are able to charge your customer.

In order to make gains in profitability, your Technicians must complete the job in a lesser time than is allocated by the manufacturer, thereby increasing Working Efficiency.

Working Efficiency is a double-edged sword. If your Technicians take more time to complete the job than the manufacturers allocated time then your profitability diminishes and working efficiency falls below 100%.

# Work-In-Progress *(Days)*

## WIP Hours ÷ N° of Tech's ÷ Hrs Attended in 1 day

### Benchmark: 3 days or less

Work in progress (WIP) simply refers to the number of hours that have been booked onto jobs that have not yet been invoiced. This vital K.P.I. informs you of the number of days Work In Progress that you have accumulated.

Example:
(A) Hours booked as WIP     = 120
(B) No of Technicians       = 6
(C) Hours Attended in 1 day = 8  (Per Technician)
(D) **Work In Progress Days = 2.5 Days**   (A ÷ B ÷ C)

Many financial reports have a tendency to provide WIP as a total monetary value, but this can often be misleading. You must ask the question, is it reporting a value based upon the Labour Cost of Sales, Hours Sold at retail value, or Hours Sold at the current Recovery Rate?

The example above just deals with the number of hours accumulated in WIP and is therefore more useful in trend analysis and deals with all eventualities.

# Interpreting Your Parts Department

**Top K.P.I's to study:**

**True Parts Stock Turn
Total Parts Stock Turn
V.O.R. %**

# Typical Parts Department Structure

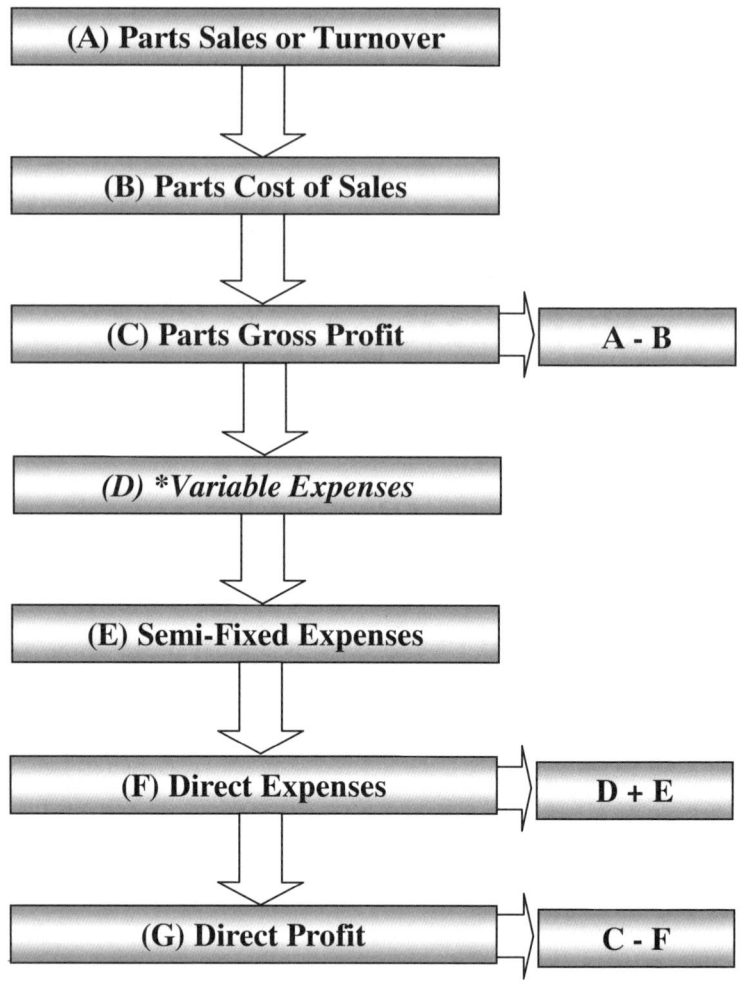

*(D) *Variable Expenses are shown in this diagram to illustrate that they are <u>not</u> generally seen within the Parts Department. This is because there is no expense that is directly attributed to the sale of every part that is sold.*

# Annualised Parts Sales

## Projected Annual Sales Volume

### Guideline: Own Policy

In order to calculate many Key Performance Indicators, your Parts Sales Volume may need to be annualised. This is simply a projection of your annual sales based on your current sales performance.

The formula is the year-to-date sales volume figure, multiplied by 12 then divided by the current month number. For example, if your current reporting period is January to April year-to-date, then the sales figure is multiplied by 12 (12 months in 1 year) and then divided by 4 (April is the $4^{th}$ month in your reporting period).

Example:
(A) January Sales = £40,652
(B) February Sales = £85,112
(C) March Sales = £60,238
(D) April Sales = £45,894
(E) Sales to date = £231,896
(F) Multiply by 12 = £2,782,752
(G) Divide by current month = 4 (April)
(H) **Annualised Sales** = **£695,688**   (F ÷ G)

This is a theoretical figure that provides you with the Sales value that you will achieve at the end of the year if your sales performance where to be maintained at the current rate.

# Average Bought Cost

## P.G. Stock + P.G. VOR Purchases ÷ P.G. Stock Value

## Guideline: Product Group Dependent

*P.G. = Product Group.*

This K.P.I. informs you of the average price that you have paid for your stock in a specific product group or specific product line.

How does this differ from your Average Buying Margin? When you sell a part there are very few systems that tell you how that specific part was ordered i.e. stock order or V.O.R? Obviously the Buying Margin in each sector is very different.

Let's say that a Parts person ordered an engine on V.O.R. for one of your key customers. The next day a different person invoices that same engine out to the customer with their regular discount terms, not knowing that the engine was ordered on V.O.R.

This scenario actually happened in real life and the dealer in question lost £95 in that instant because the amount of discount given was greater than the profit margin they had in the V.O.R. ordering system.

This K.P.I. addresses this shortfall by assessing the true price paid for each product group, thereby protecting the department against too much discount being given where parts are ordered on a V.O.R. basis.

# Average Buying Margin %

## Retail Value − Net Invoice Value ÷ Retail Value (x100)

### Guideline: Franchise Specific

This K.P.I. informs you of the average profit margin that is applied to every purchase that you have made, or in other words, it's the average amount of mark-up that you have available.

Example:
(A) Retail value of purchases = £167,822
(B) Invoice value of purchases = £110,763
(C) Average buying margin = £57,060 (A − B)
(D) **Average Buying Margin %** = **34%** (C ÷ A x 100)

This example shows that for this period, your parts purchases amounted to £110,763. If you were to sell all these parts at their full retail price the value would be £167,822 and you would be left with a Gross Profit of £57,060. (Let's not talk about discount at this stage)

The calculation is an average of all purchases made in a given period, usually 1 month, but many reports will show you the Average Buying Margin across the different product lines and product groups such as engine, brakes and filters etc.

Typically, you can find this statistic on your parts purchases reports supplied to you by your franchise manufacturer, which is usually run on a monthly basis. It is also evident on some manufacturers composite reports.

# Debtor Days

## Parts Debtors ÷ Parts Daily Credit Turnover

## Baseline < 45 days

The Debtor Days K.P.I is a measurement of the credit activity within the Parts Department. Its purpose is to inform you of the average number of days that your customers take to pay you.

Example:
(A) Parts Debtors = £40,208
(B) Parts Daily Credit Turnover* = £935
(C) **Debtor Days** = **43 days** (A ÷ B)

*Note:*
In order to calculate the Parts Daily Credit Turnover, you will need to take the annualised Parts Turnover sold on credit and divide that figure by 365 to arrive at a daily sales turnover.

Example:*
(A) Annual Turnover On Credit = £341,275
(B) Days in 1 year = 365
(C) Parts Daily Credit Turnover = £935  (A ÷ B)

In the example provided above the average amount of debt is outstanding for a period of 43 days. In many cases, customer credit agreements are for 30 days and all too often these credit terms are not fully instigated and your money is outstanding for longer periods of time. The question is how much longer?

# Departmental Expenses

## Departmental Expenses ÷ Gross Profit (x100)

## Guideline: < 40% of Gross Profit

The Departmental Expenses of the Parts Department are also known as Direct Expenses and refer to the total expenses incurred. As there are no Variable Expenses within the Parts Department, all expenses are therefore Semi-Fixed.

Typically, Departmental Expenses are shown as a monetary value and in order for you to capture meaningful trend analysis you will need to express them as a percentage of departmental Gross Profit.

Example:
(A) Departmental Expenses = £63,865
(B) Total Turnover = £187,836
(C) **Departmental Expense %** = **34%** (A ÷ B x 100)

Keeping track of your Departmental Expenses is best shown in the form of a simple graph so that you can see the trends that are emerging.

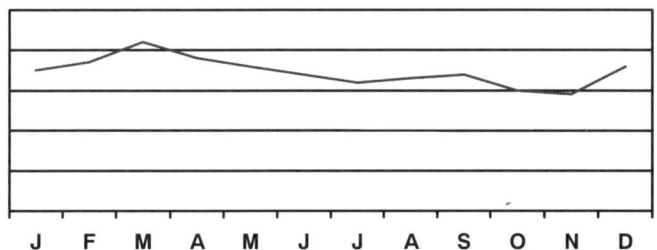

# Departmental Profit

## Gross Profit – All Departmental Expenses

## Baseline: > 12%

This line is sometimes called Direct Profit, Operating Profit, or more commonly, "the bottom line".

The mathematical formula for Departmental Profit is simply Gross Profit minus all Departmental Expenses. This is exactly the same equation as Direct Profit in the flow chart at the beginning of this section of the book.

Example:
(A) Departmental Gross Profit   = £107,539
(B) All Departmental Expenses = £82,722
(C) **Departmental Profit**        = **£24,817**  (A - B)

Departmental Profit is usually seen as the last line or the bottom line of your financial reports for the Parts Department, hence its colloquial name, "the bottom line".

However, having this figure reported as a monetary value is very nice to see, but in terms of plotting its trend, it is more useful to measure this as a percentage of Turnover.

Example:
(A) Departmental Profit        = £24,817
(B) Turnover                         = £165,446
(C) **Departmental Profit %**   = **15%**   (A ÷ B x 100)

# Direct Expenses

### Direct Expenses ÷ Gross Profit (x100)

### Guideline: < 40% of Gross Profit

The Direct Expenses of the Parts Department are also known as Departmental Expenses and refer to the total expenses incurred. Since there are no Variable Expenses within the Parts Department, all expenses are therefore Semi-Fixed.

Typically, Direct Expenses are shown as a monetary value and in order for you to capture meaningful trend analysis you will need to express them as a percentage of departmental Gross Profit.

Example:
(A) Direct Expenses     = £63,865
(B) Total Turnover       = £187,836
(C) **Direct Expense %**  = **34%** (A ÷ B x 100)

Keeping track of your Direct Expenses is best shown in the form of a simple graph so that you can see the trends that are emerging.

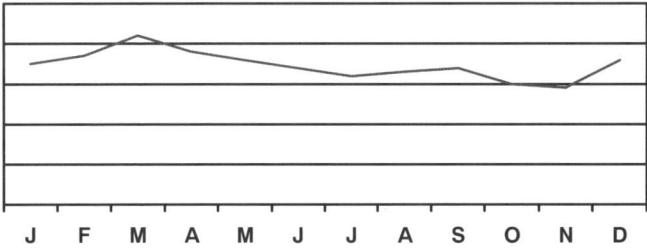

# Direct Profit

## Gross Profit – All Departmental Expenses

### Baseline: > 12% of turnover

This line is sometimes called Departmental Profit, Operating Profit, or more commonly, "the bottom line".

The mathematical formula for Direct Profit is simply Gross Profit minus all Departmental Expenses.

Example:
| | | |
|---|---|---|
| (A) Departmental Gross Profit | = | £107,539 |
| (B) All Departmental Expenses | = | £82,722 |
| (C) **Direct Profit** | = | **£24,817**  (A - B) |

Direct Profit is usually seen as the last line or the bottom line of your financial reports for the Parts Department, hence its colloquial name, "the bottom line".

However, having this figure reported as a monetary value is very nice to see, but in terms of plotting its trend, it is more useful to measure this as a percentage of Turnover.

Most financial reports now show Direct Profit as a monetary value as well as a percentage of Turnover.

Example:
| | | |
|---|---|---|
| (A) Direct Profit | = | £24,817 |
| (B) Turnover | = | £165,446 |
| (C) **Direct Profit %** | = | **15%**  (A ÷ B x 100) |

# Emergency Order %

## Purchases on E.O. ÷ Total Purchases (x 100)

### Benchmark: < 30% of purchases

E.O. is an abbreviation for Emergency Order. E.O. sales occur when a vehicle is being repaired in the workshop and the parts that are required to repair it are not currently held within your parts stock

In this instance, the required parts are ordered from your franchise manufacturer on an emergency basis and the parts are usually delivered the next day.

This K.P.I. measures the percentage of your parts purchases that have been ordered on an emergency basis.

Example:
(A) Purchases on E.O.     = £17,977
(B) Total parts purchases = £79,894
(C) **E.O. %**            = **22.5%**   (A ÷ B x 100)

In most cases, parts that are ordered on E.O carry a financial penalty, which reduces your overall Buying Margin. Therefore it is in your interest to maintain a balance between your True Stock Turn and E.O. %

# Oil & Lubricants Profitability

## Oil Gross Profit ÷ Oil Sales (x 100)

### Baseline: > 50% of Oil Sales

As an industry, we take a high profit margin from the sale of oil and lubricants. There is always a debate to be had as to whether the sale of oil and lubricants should be shown within the Service Department or the Parts Department. Some manufacturers financial reports show this statistic within the Parts Department, which provides the reason for it being shown in this section of the book, however your financial reports may show it in the Service Department.

Example:
(A) Oil Sales = £10,357
(B) Oil Cost of Sales = £3,936
(C) Oil Gross Profit = £6,421  (A – B)
(D) **Gross Profit on Oil Sales** = **62%** (C ÷ A x 100)

Most financial reports include the value of oil sales together with the value of oil gross profit; a good report will also show you the percentage of gross profit that has been retained.

*Special note:*
*In order to measure this information accurately, you need to capture the opening oil stock and the closing oil stock at the end of each period, taking into account any oil purchases and from this you can determine how much oil has been used. This of course is your true cost of sale. If you do not currently use this method, or unless your oil is metered, how is your oil being accounted for?*

# Operating Profit

## Gross Profit – All Departmental Expenses

## Baseline: > 12% of Department Turnover

This line is sometimes called Direct Profit, Departmental Profit, or more commonly, "the bottom line".

The mathematical formula for Operating Profit is simply Gross Profit minus all Departmental Expenses, this is exactly the same as Direct Profit in the flow chart at the beginning of this section of the book.

Example:
(A) Departmental Gross Profit = £107,539
(B) All Departmental Expenses = £82,722
(C) **Operating Profit** = **£24,817** (A - B)

Operating Profit is usually seen as the last line or the bottom line of your financial reports for the Parts Department, hence its colloquial name, "the bottom line".

However, having this figure reported as a monetary value is very nice to see, but in terms of plotting its trend, it is more useful to measure this as a percentage of Turnover.

Example:
(A) Operating Profit = £24,817
(B) Turnover = £165,446
(C) **Operating Profit %** = **15%** (A ÷ B x 100)

# Obsolete Stock

## Benchmark: < 1% of Stock Value

Wouldn't it be a wonderful world if you were able to sell every single part that you purchased? The truth of the matter is that you are unable to achieve this utopia in the real world and therefore you have to make decisions about how long you keep hold of stock before you admit to yourself that it's just not going to sell.

Just think for a moment about the food that you buy. Accompanying the price of the produce there is usually a date that tells you when the food must sold or it will be removed from the shelf and thrown away. This date is commonly known as the "Sell by date".

Although the parts that are occupying your shelves right now do not have a "sell by date" printed on them, you already know that there is a limited amount of time for them to sell because new vehicles are being launched and demand for older parts diminishes. Once this time has expired, those old parts are said to be past their sell by date, or in other words, they become obsolete stock.

There are no hard and fast rules for placing sell by dates on your parts stock, but the general rule seems to be around 2 years. After this amount of time, most parts have benefited from Stock Adjustments and are usually written off and thrown in the bin to make way for some fresh stock that will sell so that the profits can be recovered.

# Parts Gross Profit

## Invoice Value of Parts Sales - Parts Cost of Sales

## Guideline:  See Parts Gross Profit %

This is the invoice value of the parts sold less the cost of those parts. Generally, this is expressed as a monetary value and also as a percentage of the total sales value.

Example:
(A) Parts Sales           = £695,688
(B) Cost of Sales         = £507,852
(C) **Parts Gross Profit    = £187,836**  (A - B)

The general accounting definition for any type of Gross Profit is simply sale less cost of sale and this statistic is no exception to the rule.

The trading strategy of your Parts Department will have an impact upon the value of profit that you make and will vary according to the amount of Trade Sales, Van Sales and the value of internal discount (if any) that your business conducts.

Before you get carried away with the *value* of Gross Profit that you are generating, use this statistic in conjunction with your Gross Profit % to ensure that your business is travelling in the direction that you want it to travel.

It is possible for the value of your Gross Profit to show an increase whilst the Gross Profit % is declining. Make sure that you avoid the busy fool syndrome.

# Parts Gross Profit %

## Gross Profit ÷ Departmental Turnover (x100)

## Baseline: > 22% of Department Turnover

Financial reports for the Parts Department show Gross Profit on each individual category of Parts Sales as well as the overall total Parts Sales.

This page is explaining the total Departmental Gross Profit within which all of the individual categories are included. (Please also see Parts Sales Mix.)

Example:
(A) Total Gross Profit = £187,836
(B) Parts Sales = £695,688
(C) **Gross Profit %** = **27%**  (A ÷ B x 100)

When you express your Gross Profit as a percentage it is much easier to identify and control the direction of your department. An easy way of identifying your trading strategy is to plot a simple graph that can be updated on a monthly basis. The question that you must have the answer to is where are Rebates and Bonus accounted for?

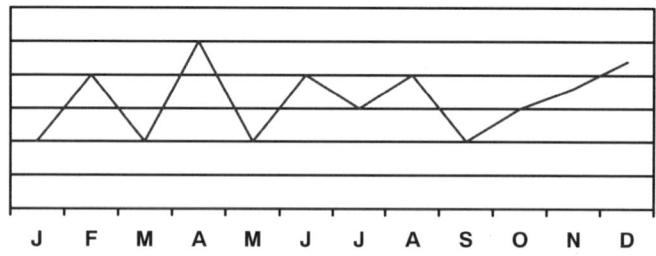

# Parts Net Profit per New Unit Sold

## Departmental Profit ÷ New Units Sold

### Guideline: Own Policy

This K.P.I is very useful in the construction of budgets and business plans when comparing your information with the national averages of your franchise. The mathematical formula is very simple and straightforward.

Example:
(A) Departmental Profit           = £75,250
(B) Number of New Vehicles Sold   = 350
(C) **Parts Profit per New Unit Sold  =  £215**  (A ÷ B)

Generally speaking, you can be reasonably accurate with a new vehicles sales volume forecast, or at least your franchise manufacturer will inform you of your territory objectives. When you have the new unit sales volume figure you can use this K.P.I. as a sanity check against your Parts Department profit objectives.

It is not possible to provide a meaningful benchmark for this K.P.I as it varies considerably across different franchises. For guidance however, a high volume franchise will produce a figure around £150 - £200 per unit, whilst a low volume or niche franchise will produce a figure that may be substantially higher.

In addition to this, your Parts Department profitability will also be affected by your trading strategy and of course the volume of Trade Sales, which have a tendency to attract higher levels of discount.

# Parts Sales

## Invoice Value of Parts Sold

## Guideline: See Parts Sales per Parc Unit

This is simply the invoice value of the parts sold. Generally, management accounts separate the different streams of income so that you can see the growth in all areas of the department.

Typically, these different categories are Retail sales, Trade sales with sales to the Service Department and Bodyshop being split between Retail, Internal and Warranty.

Many financial reports show the split of these different streams of income in the form of a simple pie chart (See Parts Sales Mix)

In order to calculate many Key Performance Indicators, Parts Sales may need to be annualised (See Annualised Parts Sales). This is simply a projection of your annual sales based on your current performance.

# Parts Sales Mix

## Category Parts Sales ÷ Total Parts Sold (x100)

## Guideline: Own Policy

This information simply informs you of the balance between the different categories into which you sell parts. In most cases the Parts Department is split into seven distinct categories of income, which are:

Retail Counter
Trade Counter
Service  - Retail
         - Internal
         - Warranty
Bodyshop
Van Sales

On most financial reports your Parts Sales Turnover is segregated into these different categories together with a percentage share of the total sales volume, sometimes in the form of a simple pie chart:

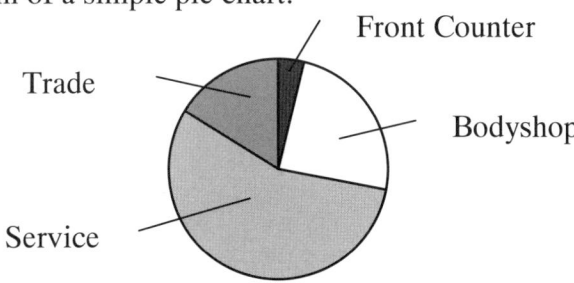

The total Parts Sales volume is usually shown after the full breakdown of these statistics.

# Parts Sales per Parc Unit

## Annual Parts Sales ÷ Number of Vehicles in Parc

## Guideline: Own Strategy

This K.P.I. is very useful for assessing your current performance in parts sales volume against your fellow dealers or your total market potential.

Example:
(A) Annualised Parts Sales = £695,688
(B) Number of vehicles in parc = 2,114
(C) **Part sold per parc unit** = **£329** (A ÷ B)

Keep in mind that this statistic is utilising every vehicle in the parc and if you are assessing a 10-year parc some of those vehicles may no longer be in your area or even in existence.

You may also wish to consider who else is registering vehicles within your territory. It could be that you have a sizeable fleet that is distorting your vehicle parc. You also have to ask yourself the question about the age profile of the vehicles that your dealership attracts.

To access the real power of this K.P.I. you will need to assess the vehicle parc for each individual year as opposed to the 10-year average. This is because the value of parts sold on a 1-year old vehicle in a 12-month period may be very different to the value of parts sold on a 4-year-old vehicle. As you can imagine, if you average this theory over a 10-year period you could end up with a sizeable distortion.

# Parts Stock Value

## Value of Parts Stock at Purchase Price

## Guideline:  See True Parts Stock Turn

This statistic simply provides you with the value of your Parts Stock at any one moment in time.

The figure is usually taken directly from your Balance Sheet from which your Parts Stock can be found within the section labelled Current Assets.

The Part Stock Value takes into account all Obsolete Stock and any parts stock write-down that has taken place within the current year and it is this figure that is used for the calculation of K.P.I's such as Parts Stock Turn.

It is important to note that this figure is reported as a monetary value and reflects the parts purchase price as opposed to the retail selling price.

The information that you really want to know here is how much stock should you be holding at any one moment in time? The answers to this question lies in the K.P.I. True Parts Stock Turn.

# Parts Sales Per Employee

## Annualised Parts Sales ÷ All Parts Personnel

### Baseline: > £250,000

This K.P.I is generally used for budgeting purposes. The calculation simply takes the Annualised Parts Turnover and divides it by the total number of people employed within the Parts Department to provide an Average Parts Sales Value Per Person.

Example:
(A) Annualised Parts Sales = £695,688
(B) Number Parts Employees = 3
(C) **Annual Sales per Employee = £231,896**  (A ÷ B)

It is important to note that the number of employees in the calculation includes everyone within the Parts Department including the Parts Manager, and not just the people who sell parts.

It is a useful statistic for ascertaining the overall utilisation of your parts personnel compared with the national average of your franchise.

You may also use it to place a sanity check on your budget. For instance, if your budget requires this K.P.I to be something in the order of £579,740 per person, then you may question whether you have sufficient people to deliver this result, or you may even question the viability of your budget.

# Rebates and Bonuses

## Guideline: Franchise Specific

Rebates and Bonuses are two different ways for a franchise manufacturer to reward a dealer for good performance.

**Rebates**. These are forms of discount that are claimed back when you hit an agreed purchase target on a specific product line or product group.

For instance, you could have a target to purchase 100 widgets at £10 each with a Rebate of £2. When you hit that target you will be able to claim the agreed Rebate of £2 on all 100 widgets that you have purchased resulting in a Rebate of £200 (100 widgets with a £2 Rebate on each). Rebates are usually retrospective upon target attainment.

**Bonuses**. These are bonus payments in the true sense of the word. Your franchise manufacturer usually provides you with an annual parts purchase target, which is broken down into quarterly segments. When you reach these targets the franchise manufacturer pays you a bonus for hitting this target.

What you need to know is this: When does the value of the Rebates and Bonus payment appear within your reports? Do they appear when you hit the target, or do they appear when you receive the payment?

This makes a considerable difference to the interpretation of your departmental profitability when you are comparing your results with everyone else.

# Semi-Fixed Expenses

## Semi-Fixed Expenses ÷ Gross Profit (x 100)

## Benchmark: < 40% of Department Turnover

The Semi-Fixed Expenses of the Parts Department refer to the total expenses incurred. As there are no expenses that are directly linked to Parts Sales volume within the Parts Department, (Variable Expenses) then all expenses are classified as Semi-Fixed.

Typically, Semi-Fixed Expenses are shown as a monetary value and in order for you to capture meaningful trend analysis you will need to express them as a percentage of Departmental Gross Profit.

Example:
(A) Departmental Expenses = £63,865
(B) Department Turnover = £187,836
(C) **Semi-Fixed Expense %** = **34%**  (A ÷ B x 100)

Keeping track of your Semi-Fixed Expenses is best shown in the form of a simple graph so that you can see the trends that are emerging.

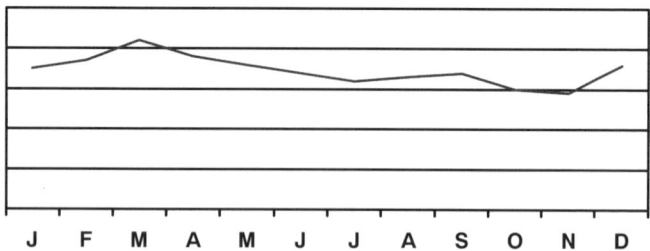

# Stock Adjustments

## Guideline: Own Policy

If there is one thing in the Motor Industry that is an absolute certainty, it is that your stock suffers the effects of depreciation on a continuous basis.

When you buy parts and sell them within a short period of time, this is when your business makes the most profit.

Obviously, the longer the parts sit on the shelf, the more depreciation they attract and the chances of selling them become fewer. If they sit there for too long, they fall into the category called Obsolete Stock.

Generally speaking, the Parts Stock holding is reviewed on an annual basis and the parts that have been in stock for some time will have a portion of their cost written off to reduce their price.

This financial write off is deducted from the profits of the Parts Department and is shown within the management accounts as an expense called Stock Adjustments.

Some businesses choose to conduct Stock Adjustments on a monthly basis, some quarterly and some annually.

There are no strict guidelines for this practice, but the more frequently you conduct the exercise, the more your attention will be focussed upon the disposal of slow moving items and of course the trend of True Parts Stock Turn.

# Total Parts Stock Turn

## Annualised Parts Purchases ÷ Stock Value

## Guideline:   Franchise Specific

When you are interested in making your money work for you, then there are two Key Performance Indicators relating to Stock Turn for you to measure: this one and True Parts Stock Turn.

It is vitally important that you understand the difference between the two K.P.I's as they tell you very different things about your business. The calculation for Total Parts Stock Turn is the Annualised Parts Purchases divided by the value of total Parts Stock.

Example:
(A) Annualised Parts Purchases         = £695,688
(B) Parts Stock Value (at cost price)    = £115,948
(C) **Total Parts Stock Turn (per year) = 6**  (A ÷ B)

This is a useful trend to measure, but it can be misleading. The assumption is that this K.P.I tells you how many times that your Parts Stock is turned over each year, whereas in reality this is not the case. This is because the total Parts Sales include sales from parts ordered on V.O.R, which are not sales from stock.

*Special note:*
*Total Parts Stock Turn is the K.P.I that is shown on most reports. When you want to measure how effectively your parts stock is being utilised then you need to measure True Parts Stock Turn.*

# True Parts Stock Turn *(Version 1)*

## Annualised Stock Purchases ÷ Stock Value

## Guideline: Franchise Specific

This is the K.P.I. that is the most valuable, useful and trustworthy when you want to measure how effective your Parts Stock is being utilised.

The calculation for True Parts Stock Turn only assesses the parts purchases for stock and excludes all parts that are purchased on a V.O.R. or E.O. basis.

Example:
(A) Annualised Stock Purchases = £486,982
(B) Annualised V.O.R. Purchases = Ignore
(C) Parts Stock Value (at cost price) = £115,948
(D) **True Parts Stock Turn (per year)** = **4.2** (A ÷ C)

This K.P.I. provides you with the true effectiveness of your Parts Stock. Quite simply, the faster your True Parts Stock Turn, the less investment is required in your stock and the more profit you will retain as a result.

Your franchise manufacturer usually provides this information to your Parts Department on a monthly basis. However, you may need to calculate the True Parts Stock Turn yourself as this is seldom shown.

# **True Parts Stock Turn** *(Version 2)*

## **Annual Sales from stock (at cost price) ÷ Stock Value**

## **Guideline:   Franchise Specific**

This version differs from version 1 on the previous page because it measures the parts that have been sold (at purchase price) rather than the parts that have simply been purchased for stock and is therefore a more accurate result.

The calculation still assesses the parts purchases for stock and excludes all parts that are purchased on a V.O.R. or E.O. basis.

Example:
(A) Annualised Sales (at cost price)   = £706,112
(B) Annual V.O.R Sales (at cost price)   = Ignore
(C) Parts Stock Value (at cost price)   = £156,913
(D) **True Parts Stock Turn (per year)**   = **4.5**  (A ÷ C)

If you are unable to obtain the purchase price of your sales, you could calculate it by using this method:

Example:
(A) Annualised Sales from stock   = £861,456
(B) Annualised V.O.R Sales   = Ignore
(C) GP on Sales from stock   = £155,344
(D) Cost price of Sales from stock = £706,112  (A - C)
(E) Parts Stock Value   = £156,913
(F) **True Parts Stock Turn**   = **4.5** (D ÷ E)

This example is the most accurate of all as it captures the exact sales and the purchases made for those sales.

# V.O.R % *(Version 1)*

## Purchases on V.O.R. ÷ All Parts Purchases (x 100)

## Benchmark: < 30% of Total Purchases

V.O.R. is an abbreviation for Vehicle Off Road. V.O.R. sales occur when a vehicle is being repaired in the workshop and the parts that are required to repair it are not currently held within your Parts Stock

In this instance, the required parts are ordered from your franchise manufacturer on an emergency basis and the parts are usually delivered the next day.

This K.P.I. measures the percentage of your parts purchases that have been ordered on an emergency basis.

Example:
(A) Purchases on V.O.R = £17,977
(B) Total parts purchases = £79,894
(C) **V.O.R. %** = **22.5%** (A ÷ B x 100)

In most cases, parts that are ordered on V.O.R carry a financial penalty, which reduces your Average Buying Margin. Therefore it is in your interest to maintain harmony and balance between your True Stock Turn and V.O.R %

The suggested Benchmark for version 1 of this K.P.I. is higher than that of version 2 because it is assessing monetary values, which can fluctuate depending upon the price of the items ordered on a V.O.R. basis.

Also see Average Bought Cost

# V.O.R % *(Version 2)*

## Total Line Items ÷ Line Items on V.O.R. (x 100)

## Benchmark: < 25% of Total Orders

The meaning of this K.P.I. is exactly the same as version 1 on the previous page, except that it measures the number of line items ordered on a V.O.R. basis as opposed to their monetary values.

Example:
(A) Line Items Ordered on V.O.R = 546
(B) Total Line Items Ordered = 2601
(C) **V.O.R. %** = **21%**  (A ÷ B x 100)

These two methods of measuring V.O.R. % are very different to each other and it is obviously critical that you know which of these versions your departmental reports are showing you.

Neither one of these methods of measuring the V.O.R % is any better than the other and neither one of them is right or wrong; it is really a matter of what you want to measure.

Both indicators are influenced by the frequency of the parts stock order that is provided by your franchise manufacturer.

The suggested benchmark for keeping VOR % less than 25% is applicable to weekly stock orders. If your stock orders are more frequent, then your VOR % should be considerably lower.

# V.O.R. Penalty

## Actual Buying Price - Optimum Terms

## Guideline: Franchise Specific

This Key Performance Indicator establishes the value of penalty that has been incurred by purchasing parts on a V.O.R. basis.

Example:
(A) Actual Buying Price = £532,423
(B) Optimum Terms Cost = £520,069
(C) **V.O.R. Penalty** = **£12,354** (A - B)

In this example, the Actual Buying Price represents the total price that you have paid for the parts that you have purchased.

The Optimum Terms Cost is the figure that you would have paid for these parts if you had ordered them all on a stock order basis.

The difference between these two values represents the additional money that you have paid to obtain these parts on the V.O.R. ordering system.

The value of this penalty is dependent upon your Parts Sales, V.O.R. %, and of course the frequency of your parts deliveries.

Measuring the value of the V.O.R. Penalty can be misleading when comparing your information with other businesses so to level out the playing field in this area refer to the V.O.R. Penalty % on the following page.

# V.O.R. Penalty %

## V.O.R. Penalty ÷ Parts List Price (x100)

## Guideline: Franchise Specific

This Key Performance Indicator is most effective for measuring the trend of your V.O.R. Penalty, especially when comparing your results with other dealers.

Example:
(A) V.O.R. Penalty*  = £12,354
(B) Purchases at List Price  = £734,743
(C) **V.O.R. Penalty %**  = **1.68%**  (A ÷ B)

\* Please see V.O.R. Penalty on the previous page to gain a full understanding of this equation.

In this example, Purchases at List Price represent the total price that you would receive if you were to sell all the parts at their full retail sales value.

Although you will not receive the full list price due to the discount that you give on some parts sales, it is the best yardstick to use as a comparison because different dealers give different levels of discount. If you used your parts sales turnover for this equation, the different levels of discount would produce a sizeable distortion.

Your franchise manufacturer usually provides your Parts Department with these statistics on a monthly basis.

Also see Average Bought Cost

# Interpreting Your Bodyshop

**Top Tips to study:**

**Productivity
Recovery Rate
Estimate Conversion Ratio**

# Typical Bodyshop Structure

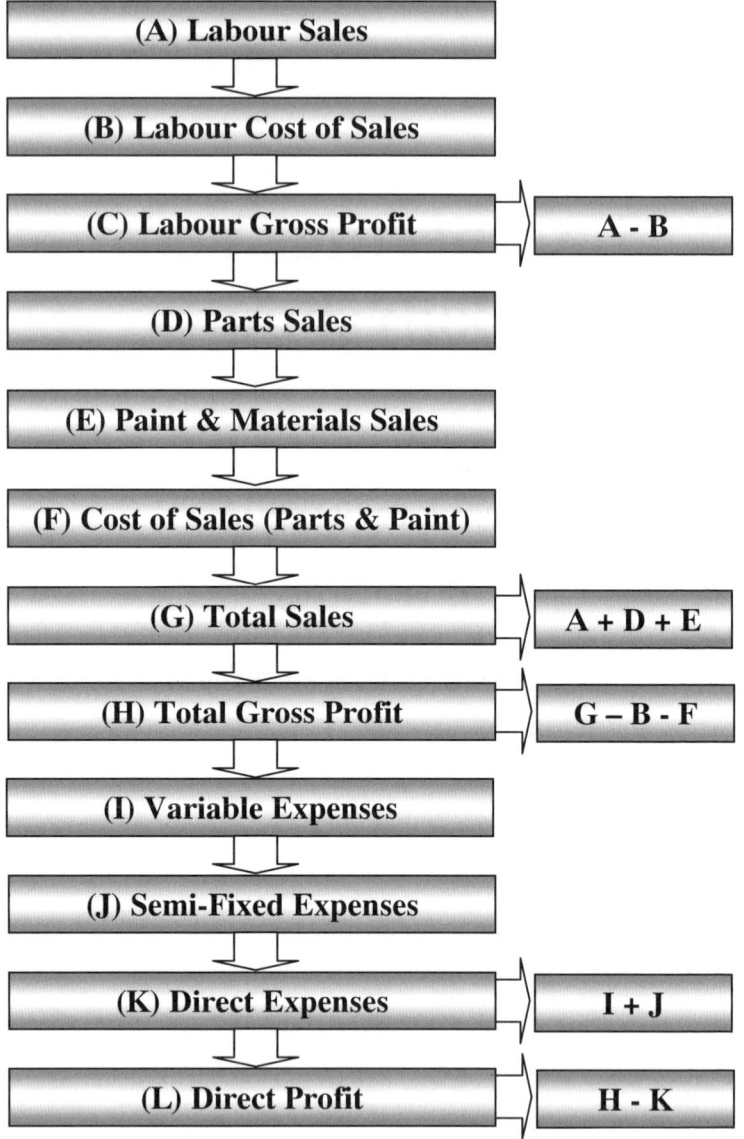

# Debtor Days

## Bodyshop Debtors ÷ Bodyshop Daily Credit Turnover

## Benchmark: < 45 days

The Debtor Days K.P.I is a measurement of the credit activity within the Bodyshop. Its purpose is to inform you of the average number of days that your customers take to pay you.

Example:
(A) Bodyshop Debtors = £126,591
(B) Daily Credit Turnover* = £2,943
(C) **Debtor Days** = **43 days** (A ÷ B)

*Note:*
In order to calculate the Bodyshop Daily Credit Turnover, you will need to take the annualised Bodyshop Turnover sold on credit and divide that figure by 365 to arrive at a daily sales turnover.

Example:*
(A) Annual Turnover On Credit = £1,074,195
(B) Days in 1 year = 365
(C) Bodyshop Daily Credit Turnover = £2,943 (A ÷ B)

In many cases, customer credit agreements are for 30 days and all too often these credit terms are not fully instigated and your money is outstanding for longer periods of time. An increasing problem within this sector of business is the value of Debtors owed by insurance companies. Due to very lean trading margins, it is critical to keep control of this Key Performance Indicator.

# Departmental Expenses

## Departmental Expenses ÷ Turnover (x100)

### Guideline: Own Policy

The Departmental Expenses of the Bodyshop are also known as Direct Expenses and refer to the total expenses incurred. They represent the sum total of the Variable Expenses and Semi-Fixed Expenses.

Typically, Departmental Expenses are shown as a monetary value and in order for you to capture meaningful trend analysis you will need to express them as a percentage of departmental Turnover.

Example:
(A) Variable Expenses = £28,655
(B) Semi-Fixed Expenses = £143,272
(C) **Departmental Expenses** = **£171,927** (A + B)
(D) Department Turnover = £573,088
(E) **Departmental Expense %** = **30%** (C ÷ D x 100)

Keeping control of Departmental Expenses can be a difficult task unless you fully understand the difference between Variable Expenses and Semi-Fixed Expenses.

Variable Expenses are directly linked to sales volume and Semi-Fixed Expenses are not linked to sales volume therefore the actions that you need to take to maintain control is different in each area.

# Departmental Profit %

**Departmental Profit ÷ Turnover (x100)**

**Baseline: > 30%**

The Departmental Profit of the Bodyshop is also called many other things such as, Direct Profit, Operating Profit and of course the bottom line.

You may have already deduced from the financial structure of the department at the beginning of this section that Departmental Profit is calculated by taking Gross Profit minus Departmental Expenses. To make sense of this figure it is always expressed as a percentage of Turnover when used for trending as it is the direction of travel that is of most interest to you.

Example:
(A) Departmental Profit           = £183,389
(B) Departmental Turnover     = £573,088
(C) **Departmental Profit %**     = **32%**   (A ÷ B x 100)

Keeping track of your Departmental Profit % is best shown in the form of a simple graph that is updated monthly so that you can see the trends that are emerging.

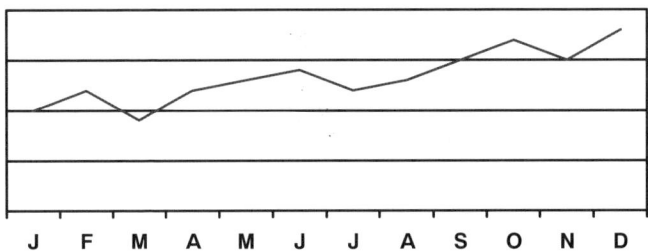

# Direct Expenses

## Departmental Expenses ÷ Turnover (x100)

### Guideline: Own Policy

The Direct Expenses of the Bodyshop are also known as Departmental Expenses and refer to the total expenses incurred. They represent the sum total of the Variable Expenses and Semi-Fixed Expenses.

Typically, Direct Expenses are shown as a monetary value and in order for you to capture meaningful trend analysis you will need to express them as a percentage of departmental Turnover.

Example:
(A) Variable Expenses = £28,655
(B) Semi-Fixed Expenses = £143,272
(C) **Direct Expenses** = **£171,927** (A + B)
(D) Department Turnover = £573,088
(E) **Direct Expense %** = **30%** (C ÷ D x 100)

Keeping control of Direct Expenses can be a difficult task unless you fully understand the difference between Variable Expenses and Semi-Fixed Expenses.

Variable Expenses are directly linked to sales volume and Semi-Fixed Expenses are not linked to sales volume therefore the actions that you need to take to maintain control is different in each area.

# Direct Profit %

## Direct Profit ÷ Turnover (x100)

### Guideline: > 30%

The Direct Profit of the Bodyshop is also called many other things such as, Departmental Profit, Operating Profit and of course the bottom line.

Direct Profit is calculated by taking Gross Profit minus Departmental Expenses. To make sense of this figure it is always expressed as a percentage of Turnover when used for trending as it is the direction of travel that is of most interest to you.

Example:
(A) Direct Profit           = £183,389
(B) Departmental Turnover   = £573,088
(C) **Direct Profit %**     = **32%**   (A ÷ B x 100)

Keeping track of your Direct Profit % is best shown in the form of a simple graph that is updated monthly so that you can see the trends that are emerging.

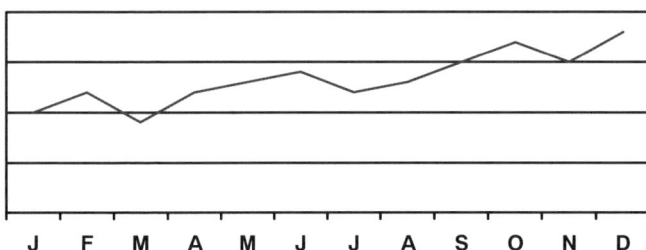

# Diverted Time

## Hours Attended – Hours Worked

### Guideline: See Utilisation

This term is also known as Unrecovered Time, or Idle Time.

Diverted Time means that the Productives have been diverted onto tasks that cannot be charged out to the customer. Typically this could be time spent locating a vehicle, waiting for parts and other such issues.

Example:
(A) Hours Attended = 320
(B) Hours Worked = 304
(C) **Hours Diverted = 16** (A - B)
(D) Prime labour Cost = £10
(E) **Diverted Time = £160** (C x D)

The mathematical formula is simply Hours Attended minus Hours Worked and this is always shown as a monetary value, which can usually be found within the Variable Expenses of the Bodyshop.

In addition to this some financial reports might show the monetary value of Diverted Time as a percentage of the Departmental Gross Profit.

(Also see Hours Attended and Hours Worked)

# Estimate Conversion Ratio

## N° of Jobs from Estimates ÷ N° of Estimates (x100)

### Baseline: > 80%

This K.P.I. assesses how many jobs you have gained from the estimates that you have given.

Example:
(A) N° of jobs from estimates = 262
(B) N° of estimates given = 304
(C) **Estimate Conversion Ratio = 0.86:1**   (A ÷ B)

More often than not, this K.P.I. is referred to as a ratio, but in terms of reporting format it is usually displayed as a percentage.

The measurement is exactly the same the only difference is that you multiply the result by 100 to convert the ratio into a percentage. It's really a matter of your preference.

Example:
(A) N° of jobs from estimates = 262
(B) N° of estimates given = 304
(C) **Estimate Conversion % = 86%**  (A ÷ B x 100)

In simplistic terms these examples show that for every estimate that you have provided, you have successfully converted 86% of them into jobs for your business.

# Gross Profit %

## Gross Profit ÷ Turnover (x100)

### Baseline: > 45%

Within the Bodyshop there are two levels of Gross Profit that are measured; be sure that you are measuring the results that you really want.

Financial reports for the Bodyshop show Gross Profit on Labour Sales before they show the total Departmental Gross Profit; this page is explaining the overall Departmental Gross Profit within which Labour Gross Profit is included. *(Please also see Labour Gross Profit.)*

The basic concept of Gross Profit is simply sale less cost of sale, therefore the following example relates to the Bodyshop as a whole.

Example:
(A) Total Gross Profit = £298,006
(B) Turnover = £573,088
(C) **Gross Profit %** = **52%** (A ÷ B x 100)

The trading strategy of your Bodyshop will have an impact upon the suggested baseline of 45% and will vary according to the level of insurance work that your business undertakes.

The Gross Profit % of a Bodyshop has a tendency to be lower than that of the Service Department because of lower Recovery Rates and higher Productive Labour costs.

# Hours Attended

## Total Number of Productive Hours Available

## Guideline: See Hours Bought

This term represents the total number of hours that the Productive staff are available to work, or in other words, the total number of hours that the Productives are clocked-in at the dealership.

The number of Hours Attended is the statistic that is used in the calculation of Utilisation and Overall Efficiency.

It is important to note that this does not give you the total number of Hours Worked; it provides you with the total number of hours that are *Available* to work.

As well as collating the total number of Hours Attended, it is also recommended that you calculate the hours attended for each individual Productive so that's their own individual Utilisation can be ascertained.

Factors that will influence the number of Hours Attended is time spent on training courses, time off on holiday, and sickness.

# Hours Bought

## Total Number of Hours Paid to Productive Personnel

### Guideline:  See Hours Attended

This term represents the total number of hours that you pay your Productives, or in other words, it represents the total Productives salary for the specified period.

It includes time spent at the dealership, time spent on training courses, sickness and holiday pay.

Example:
| | | | |
|---|---|---|---|
| (A) Training | = | 80 hours | (2 weeks) |
| (B) Holiday | = | 160 Hours | (4 weeks) |
| (C) Sickness | = | 40 hours | (1 week) |
| (D) Attended Hours | = | 1800 | (45 weeks) |
| (E) **Total Hours Bought** | **=** | **2080** | (52 weeks) |

For statistical purposes, and the calculation of key performance indicators, Hours Bought is never considered in any equation. For the most part, it is usually seen in business plans and annual budgets so that an accurate forecast of costs can be attained.

For instance, there are fifty-two weeks in the year of which four weeks could be allocated to holiday, two weeks allocated to training, and one week could be allocated for sickness.

Simply by multiplying the hourly rate that you pay to your Productives you are able to calculate a reasonably accurate forecast in each sector listed.

# Hours per Vehicle Parc

## Annualised Hours Sold ÷ Number of Vehicles in Parc

### Guideline: Own Strategy

This K.P.I. is very useful for assessing your current performance in hours sold against your fellow dealers or your total market penetration.

Example:
(A) Annual hours sold = 91,008
(B) Number of vehicles in parc = 7,584
(C) **Hours sold per parc vehicle** = **12** (A ÷ B)

Keep in mind that this statistic is utilising every vehicle in the parc and if you are assessing a 10-year parc some of those vehicles may no longer be in your area or even in existence.

You may also wish to consider who else is registering vehicles within your territory it could be that you have a sizeable fleet that is distorting your vehicle parc. You also have to ask yourself the question about the age profile of the vehicles that your business attracts.

Many financial reports also show you an average repair figure per vehicle in your parc, which uses an incident rate of around 20% and splits the hours between insurance and non-insurance work. This will provide you with a more realistic and accurate figure with which to obtain your territory potential.

# Hours Sold

### Total Number of Hours Invoiced

### Guideline:  See Labour Sales Mix

This figure represents the total number of hours that have been invoiced. Of course, the monetary value of this statistic is represented by the Labour Sales value.

It is more important to keep track of the number of Hours Sold than it is to keep track of their monetary value. This is because the monetary value of the Hours Sold can be influenced by your charge out rate and Recovery Rate and this does not therefore provide you with an accurate reflection of the direction of your business.

By far the easiest way to track the performance of the Hours Sold is to compile them into a simple graph on a weekly or monthly basis.

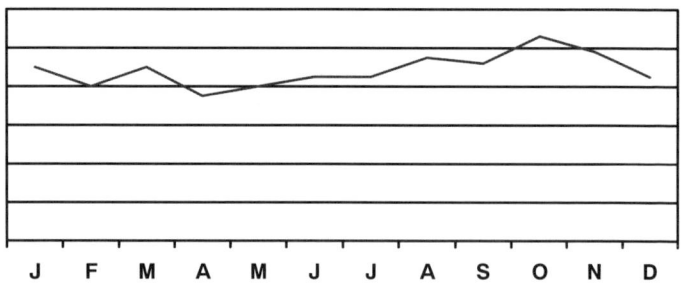

The graph will of course be more meaningful if you are able to segregate the hours sold between Retail, Internal, Insurance and Warranty so that you can accurately plot the trend in each performance sector.

# Hours Sold per Repair

**Insurance Hours Sold ÷ Number of Insurance Repairs**

**Baseline: > 18 Hours**

This K.P.I generally deals with work carried out for insurance companies, as they tend to be the larger accident repair jobs.

The equation simply divides the number of Hours Sold by the number of repairs to provide you with an average number of hours per repair.

Example:
(A) Insurance Hours Sold        = 968
(B) Number of Insurance Repairs = 51
(C) **Hours Sold per Repair**       = **19**  (A ÷ B)

The resulting K.P.I. gives you an indication of the type of work that you are receiving from your insurance companies and is also a measurement of the skills of your Estimator.

If your reported figures are below the suggested baseline of 18 hours it could be that you are receiving more of the smaller type of repairs or it could be that the Estimator is falling short of requirements.

# Hours Worked

## Hours Attended – Idle Time

## Guideline: See Utilisation

This statistic represents the number of hours that the Productives have been working productively.

Working productively means, panel beating, spraying or trimming or in other words, working on time that can be charged out to the customer.

Although a Productive may be clocked in and available to work for 40 hours per week, the time that they spent working productively is shown as the Hours Worked.

Example:
(A) Hours Attended = 40
(B) Idle Time = 2
(C) **Hours Worked = 38** (A - B)

There is only one way to accurately capture the number of Hours Worked productively and that is for each Productive to clock on and off each individual job.

Whatever your thoughts in this area of analysis there is one question that must be asked. If you do not accurately record this key performance area, when you do have a problem that you want to resolve, where do you begin to look for the answers? There is an old quote that says:
"If you can't measure it, you can't manage it."

# Idle Time

## Hours Attended – Hours Worked

## Guideline: See Utilisation

This term is also known as Unrecovered Time, or Diverted Time.

Idle Time does not mean that the Productives are standing around idle; it simply represents the time spent at the business that cannot be charged out to the customer.

Typically this could be time spent locating a vehicle, waiting for parts and other such issues.

Example:
(A) Hours Attended   = 320
(B) Hours Worked     = 304
(C) **Hours Idle**       = **16**   (A - B)
(D) Prime labour Cost = £10
(E) **Idle Time**        = **£160** (C x D)

The mathematical formula is simply Hours Attended minus Hours Worked and this is always shown as a monetary value, which can usually be found within the Variable Expenses of the Bodyshop.

In addition to this, some financial reports might show the monetary value of Idle Time as a percentage of the Departmental Gross Profit.

(Also see Hours Attended and Hours Worked)

# Labour Cost of Sales

## Value of Hours Attended - Idle Time

## Baseline: 90% of Attended Hours

This statistic captures the amount of money that is paid to Productives for every hour that is worked productively.

The amount of money that you pay your Productives per hour is divided into three sections: Hours Attended, Hours Worked Productively and Idle Time.

Hours Attended simply represents the number of hours that the Productives have been clocked in and available to work, these hours are simply divided between Hours Worked Productively and Idle Time.

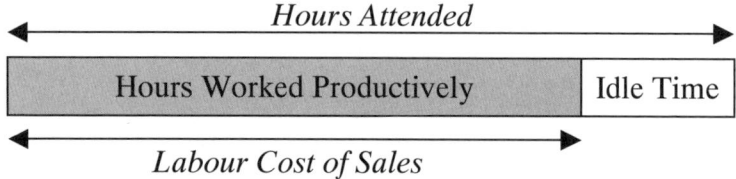

This example demonstrates that the cost of labour for the hours that have been sold can only be the hours spent working productively, and therefore Idle Time (or Diverted Time) is shown as a Variable Expense.

Example:
(A) Value of Hours Attended   = £6,290
(B) Idle Time                 = £320
(C) **Labour Cost of Sales**  = **£5,970**   (A - B)

# Labour Efficiency %

## Hours Worked ÷ Hours Attended (x100)

## Benchmark: 85% - 95%

This K.P.I is also known as Utilisation, Labour Utilisation and Selling Efficiency. The statistic tells you how much of the Productives Attended time is actually spent working productively.

In more simplistic terms, each Productive usually clocks in and is available for eight hours each day, but how much of that time is spent spray-gun-in-hand or panel beating or in other words, working on hours that can be charged out to the customer? Labour Efficiency gives you the answer to this question.

Example:
(A) Hours Worked = 957
(B) Hours Attended = 1,040
(C) **Labour Efficiency** = **92%**   (A ÷ B x 100)

This example shows that the Productives have attended 1,040 hours at the dealership of which 92% of that time has been spent working productively. The remaining 8% will be shown in your expenses as Idle Time.

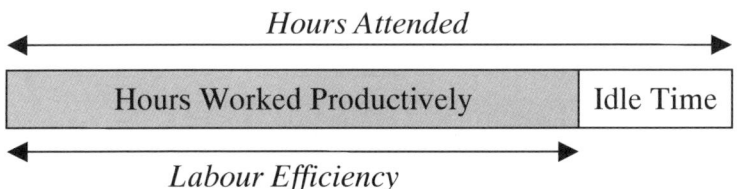

# Labour Gross Profit

## Labour Sales - Labour Cost of Sales

## Guideline: See Labour Gross Profit %

This is probably one of the most misunderstood calculations of all and is therefore worthy of your full consideration.

Most people are of the assumption that the Labour Gross Profit is Labour Sales minus Hours Attended. If this were to be the case Diverted Time would be reported at zero.

The true calculation is the monetary value of the Hours Sold minus the monetary value of the Hours Worked productively.

Example:
(A) Labour Sales *(hours sold)* = £42,240
(B) Hours Worked Productively = £7,803
(C) **Labour Gross Profit** = **£34,437** (A – B)

It is important to note here that the Labour Cost of Sales is only the value of the hours spent working productively on the hours that have been sold. You can deduce from this calculation that the Productives time is split between hours worked productively and Idle Time.

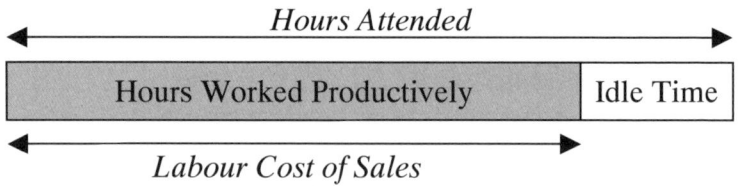

# Labour Gross Profit %

## Labour Gross Profit ÷ Labour Sales (x 100)

### Baseline: > 65%

Before you read this page, please read Labour Gross Profit to ensure that you have the true understanding of the performance area that your are measuring.

All profit-related K.P.I's are usually measured against Turnover, and in this instance the starting figure for your profit retention in the Bodyshop is 65%.

Example:
(A) Labour Gross Profit   =   £182,241
(B) Labour Sales   =   £253,112
(C) **Labour Gross Profit  =  72%**   (A ÷ B x 100)

It is important to maintain a high profit margin in this K.P.I. because the Departmental Expenses erode much of it away. Therefore if your performance in this area is below 65%, you will struggle to achieve a reasonable level of profitability when you reach the Direct Profit of your Bodyshop.

This statistic has a tendency to be lower than that of the Service Department due to lower Recovery Rates and higher Productive costs.

# Labour Sales per Parc Unit

## Annualised Labour Sales ÷ Vehicles in Parc

## Guideline: Own Policy

This is a key performance indicator that you need to thoroughly examine and fully understand before you make any judgements whatsoever as it makes some far-reaching assumptions. Its purpose it to ascertain the value of Labour Sales that you are achieving as an average across your vehicle parc.

Example:
(A) Annualised Labour Sales = £664,848
(B) Vehicle Parc = 1,560
(C) **Labour Sales Per Parc Unit** = **£426**  (A ÷ B)

This example shows that for every vehicle in the parc you are currently achieving an average Labour Sales value of £426.

Different manufacturers account for vehicle parc over different spans of time. For instance, some manufacturers use a five-year parc, some use a seven-year parc and others use a ten-year parc.

Also note that the age span of vehicle parc for the Bodyshop is often different to that of the Service and Parts Departments. Be sure to obtain the correct interpretation from your respective manufacturer.

This statistic is not to be used to assess territory potential because it is taking your current labour sales as opposed to what could be achieved.

# Labour Sales Mix

## (Sector) Hours Sold ÷ Total Hours Sold (x100)

## Guideline: See Hours Sold

This information simply informs you of the sectors into which you are selling hours.

In the case of franchised dealers, the Labour Sales Mix for the Bodyshop is split into three distinct categories of income sectors, which are Retail, Internal, and Warranty.

In the case of a stand-alone independent Bodyshop, the Labour Sales Mix may be split between, Retail, Insurance, Franchised Dealers and Fleet.

Whatever your circumstances, you may see your Labour Sales Mix being displayed as a Pie Chart to give an instant picture of your status.

However, it is always wise to measure your Labour Sales Mix in Hours Sold as opposed to the monetary value of Labour Sales because Recovery Rates vary across each income sector as do the charge out rates.

Price differences lead to inconsistency when measuring the trend and direction of your Bodyshop and it is therefore more meaningful to measure the Hours Sold into each income sector. All of the price differences and distortions are eradicated when the number of Hours Sold are analysed as opposed to their monetary values.

(Also see Retail:Insurance Ratio)

# Labour Utilisation %

## Hours Worked ÷ Hours Attended (x100)

## Baseline: 85% - 95%

This K.P.I is also known as Utilisation, Labour Efficiency and Selling Efficiency. The statistic tells you how much of the Productives Attended time is actually spent working productively.

In more simplistic terms, each Productive usually clocks in and is available for eight hours each day, but how much of that time is spent spray-gun-in-hand or panel beating, working on hours that can be charged out to the customer? Labour Utilisation gives you the answer to this question.

Example:
(A) Hours Worked = 957
(B) Hours Attended = 1,040
(C) **Labour Utilisation** = **92%**  (A ÷ B x 100)

This example shows that the Productives have Attended 1,040 hours at the dealership of which 92% of that time has been spent working productively. The remaining 8% will be shown in your expenses as Idle Time (or Diverted Time).

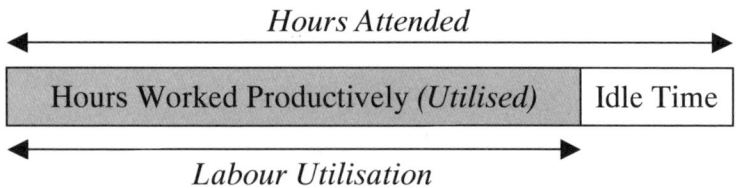

# Lead Time

**"I want my vehicle repaired, when can you do it?"**

**Benchmark: 7 days or less**

The Lead Time is the length of time a customer must wait before your Bodyshop can repair their vehicle.

A short Lead Time is usually expected and generally accepted by a customer unless they have a serious problem that needs immediate attention.

A long Lead Time of ten days or more is not generally understood or accepted by a customer and usually results in them taking their vehicle elsewhere to be repaired.

Factors that affect the length of Lead Time are Utilisation, customer retention, and marketing activity.

The length of Lead Time that your Bodyshop has is really a reflection of the work that is available to you and your ability to cope with its demand.

If your Lead Time is ten days or more on a consistent basis, then you should certainly examine your Utilisation or even your policy regarding courtesy cars.

If your Lead Time is nonexistent on a continual basis, then your marketing campaigns may need an extra boost to gain additional work.

# Lost Time

## Hours Attended – Hours Worked

## Guideline:  See Utilisation

This term is also known as Unrecovered Time, Idle Time or Diverted Time.

Lost Time means that the Productives have been diverted onto tasks that cannot be charged out to the customer and as such the chargeable time is therefore lost. Typically this could be time spent locating a vehicle, waiting for parts and other such issues.

Example:
(A) Hours Attended = 320
(B) Hours Worked = 304
(C) **Hours Lost** = **16**   (A - B)
(D) Prime labour Cost = £10
(E) **Lost Time** = **£160**   (C x D)

The mathematical formula is simply Hours Attended minus Hours Worked and this is always shown as a monetary value, which can usually be found within the Variable Expenses of the Bodyshop.

In addition to this some financial reports might show the monetary value of Lost Time as a percentage of the Departmental Gross Profit.

(Also see Hours Attended and Hours Worked)

# Operating Profit %

## Operating Profit ÷ Turnover (x100)

### Baseline: > 30%

The Operating Profit of the Bodyshop is also called many other things such as, Direct Profit, and of course the bottom line.

Operating Profit is exactly the same as Departmental Profit and is calculated by taking Gross Profit minus Departmental Expenses. To make sense of this figure it is always expressed as a percentage of Turnover when used for trending as it is the direction of travel that is of most interest to you.

Example:
(A) Operating Profit = £183,389
(B) Departmental Turnover = £573,088
(C) **Operating Profit %** = **32%** (A ÷ B x 100)

Keeping track of your Operating Profit % is best shown in the form of a simple graph that is updated monthly so that you can see the trends that are emerging.

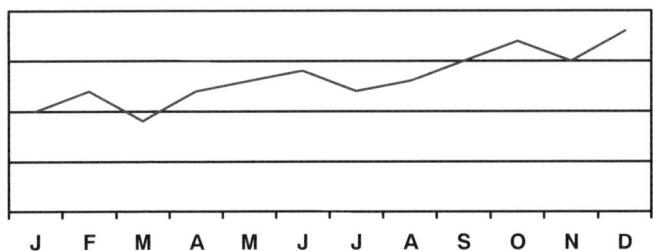

# Overall Efficiency %

## Hours Sold ÷ Hours Attended (x100)

### Baseline: 105%

This K.P.I measures the relationship between the number of hours that have been sold and the number of hours that the Productives have been available to work.

Example:
(A) Hours Sold = 1,130
(B) Hours Attended = 1,040
(C) **Overall Efficiency** = **108%**   (A ÷ B x 100)

This example shows that the Bodyshop has successfully sold more hours than the Productives have Attended, therefore the Overall Efficiency of the department is in excess of 100%.

The direction and travel of this key performance indicator keeps you informed of the balance and harmony that must exist between your Utilisation and Productivity.

Overall Efficiency clearly demonstrates that there is little point in increasing one and ignoring the other.

Example:
(A) Utilisation = 92%
(B) Productivity = 114%
(C) **Overall Efficiency** = **104.88%**   (A x B ÷ 100)

# Paint & Materials per Labour Hour

## Value of Paint & Materials ÷ Hours Sold (x100)

### Guideline: Franchise Specific

This K.P.I takes the invoice value of the Paint & Materials that you have sold and divides it by the total number of Hours Sold to provide you with an average value of paint & materials per hour.

Example:
(A) Value of Paint & Materials = £8,136
(B) Hours Sold = 1,130
(C) **Paint & Materials / Hour = £7.20** (A ÷ B)

This example simply shows that for every hour that you have invoiced, you have sold Paint & Materials to the average value of £7.20.

If your reported K.P.I. is reported lower than the national average it could be that you may have a problem with your invoicing procedures and some paint and materials are escaping the invoice.

Some reports separate this K.P.I. to show paint and materials as a different value, it's all a matter of what you want to measure.

# Parts Sales per Labour Hour

## Parts Sales to the Bodyshop ÷ Hours Sold

### Guideline: Own Policy

This K.P.I. produces a monetary figure that is the average value of parts sold for every labour hour that is sold.

It provides you with an indication of whether your Bodyshop is working with minor accident repairs with few parts being issued or the more lucrative larger jobs such as major accident repairs where more expensive parts are being used.

Example:
(A) Parts Sales to the Bodyshop = £42,240
(B) Hours Sold = 870
(C) **Parts Sales per Labour Hour = £48.55**  (A ÷ B)

Hypothetically, let's say that your K.P.I. in this area is less than the national average. This might suggest that your Bodyshop is working with smaller jobs that require fewer parts.

On the other hand if your reported K.P.I. is higher than the national average this might suggest that your Bodyshop is conducting more major bodywork jobs and thereby fitting more parts for each hour sold.

This is a useful K.P.I. for getting to grips with the type of work that you are doing and it is also very useful in the preparation of your budgets and business plans.

# Policy Costs

**"Certainly, we'll rectify that for you right now."**

**Guideline: Own Policy**

This term is also known as Policy Adjustments, Goodwill or Rectification. It refers to those costs that must be borne by the Bodyshop that cannot be reclaimed or charged on to warranty or any other Department.

Let's say that three days ago you repaired a vehicle and now the customer has returned to you because one of the doors is not fitting properly.

Naturally, you cannot expect the customer to pay any more money, as they have already paid for the job. Therefore you agree to rectify the problem for the customer, and the question is who pays the bill?

Since this job is the direct responsibility of the Bodyshop, it cannot be charged onto warranty or any other department and therefore the hours spent on the rectification is accounted for within Policy Costs in your management accounts.

Whilst this is a simplistic explanation, the same holds true for any other work that you conduct that cannot be charged elsewhere.

The time may come where you may choose to rectify some work on a customer's vehicle that is not of your doing and you offer to do the work as a gesture of goodwill.

# Productive Efficiency %

## Hours Sold ÷ Hours Worked Productively (x100)

### Benchmark: 105% to 115%

This K.P.I. is also known as Productivity and Working Efficiency. It shows you the Productives ability to complete their work within the agreed hours provided by the Estimator.

This statistic is not as straightforward as the Service Department equation, as due to the nature of the work it is not possible for a franchise manufacturer to apportion standard times.

Example:
(A) Hours Sold = 1,083
(B) Hours Worked productively = 958
(C) **Productive Efficiency** = **113%** (A ÷ B x 100)

When a customer brings a vehicle to your Bodyshop for repair you provide them with an estimate that states the number of hours to be charged. This allocated time is the maximum amount that you are able to charge.

In order to make gains in profitability, your Productives must complete the job in a lesser time than is allocated by the Estimator, thereby increasing your Productive Efficiency %.

Productive Efficiency is a double-edged sword. If you take more time to complete the job then your Productive Efficiency falls below 100%.

# Productive Ratio

## Productive staff ÷ Non-Productive staff

## Guideline: 2:1

This K.P.I. measures the ratio between productive staff and non-productive staff.

Typically, non-productive staff could be the Bodyshop Manager, Administration and Receptionist

Example:
(A) Productive staff      = 12
(B) Non-Productive staff  = 6
(C) **Productive Ratio**  = **2:1**  (A ÷ B)

Composite results appear to average at around 2:1, or in other words, for every 2 Productives that you employ, you have 1 member of staff who is non-productive.

This ratio can vary wildly and is dependant upon how you apportion your Apprentices and Foreman. There are also differences between a franchised Bodyshop and an Independent body repairer.

In any event, make sure that you understand what you are looking at when you read this information as some financial reports show this equation in reverse.

# Productivity %

## Hours Sold ÷ Hours Worked Productively (x100)

### Benchmark: 105% to 115%

This K.P.I. is also known as Productive Efficiency or Working Efficiency. It shows you the Productives ability to complete their work within the agreed hours provided by the Estimator.

This statistic is not as straightforward as the Service Department equation, as due to the nature of the work it is not possible for a franchise manufacturer to apportion standard times.

Example:
(A) Hours Sold = 1,083
(B) Hours Worked productively = 958
(C) **Productivity** = **113%**   (A ÷ B x 100)

When a customer brings a vehicle to your Bodyshop for repair you provide them with an estimate that states the number of hours to be charged. This allocated time is the maximum amount that you are able to charge.

In order to make gains in profitability, your Productives must complete the job in a lesser time than is allocated by the Estimator, thereby increasing your Productivity.

Productivity is a double-edged sword. If you take more time to complete the job then your Productivity falls below 100%.

# Productive Staff : Non-Productive Staff

## Productive staff ÷ Non-Productive staff

## Guideline: 2:1

This K.P.I. measures the ratio between productive staff and non-productive staff and is sometimes called the Productive Ratio.

Typically, non-productive staff could be the Bodyshop Manager and Receptionist.

Example:
(A) Productive staff = 12
(B) Non-Productive staff = 6
(C) **Productive : Non Productive** = **2:1**  (A ÷ B)

Composite results appear to average at around 2:1, or in other words, for every 2 Productives that you employ, you have 1 member of staff who is non-productive.

This ratio can vary wildly and is dependant upon how you apportion your Apprentices and Foreman. There are also differences between a franchised Bodyshop and an Independent.

In any event, make sure that you understand what you are looking at when you read this information as some financial reports show this equation in reverse.

# Recovery Rate

## Labour Sales ÷ Hours Sold

## Guideline: Dependent upon Insurance Content

Your Bodyshop will have a published labour rate per hour, but how often are you able to charge this amount to every customer on every job?

Recovery Rate tells you how much revenue you have <u>actually</u> recovered per hour sold as opposed to how much you would have generated should you have applied your full charge out rate.

Example:
(A) Labour Sales   = £33,731
(B) Hours Sold     = 875
(C) **Recovery Rate** = **£38.55**   (A ÷ B)

The reality of the situation confirms that you are often forced to provide a discount in some instances, especially to Insurance Companies, which of course reduces the amount of revenue that you are able to collect. The question is how much money have you managed to recover?

The key to success with this K.P.I is to capture individual Recovery Rates for each income sector (See Labour Sales Mix) so that you can accurately pinpoint the areas in which discount is being given.

# Rectification

## "Certainly, we'll rectify that for you right now."

### Guideline: Own Policy

This term is also known as Policy Adjustments, Policy Costs or Goodwill. It refers to those costs that must be borne by the Bodyshop that cannot be reclaimed or charged on to warranty or any other Department.

Let's say that three days ago you repaired a vehicle and now the customer has returned to you because one of the doors is not fitting properly.

Naturally, you cannot expect the customer to pay any more money, as they have already paid for the job. Therefore you agree to rectify the problem for the customer, and the question is who pays the bill?

Since this job is the direct responsibility of the Bodyshop, it cannot be charged onto warranty or any other department and therefore the hours spent on the rectification is accounted for within Rectification or Goodwill within your management accounts.

Whilst this is a simplistic explanation, the same holds true for any other work that you conduct that cannot be charged elsewhere.

# Repair Orders per Productive

## Number of Repair Orders ÷ Number of Productives

### Guideline: Own Policy

This is another of those key performance indicators that is used to level the playing field when comparing one business with another.

It removes the emotion of the big numbers that may be involved and produces an average number of jobs that an individual Productive undertakes in a given period.

Example:
(A) Total Repair Orders = 1,458
(B) Number of Productives = 6
(C) **Repair Orders per Productive** = **243**  (A ÷ B)

There are a multitude of factors that will affect this statistic including Productivity, Utilisation, and the type of work being undertaken and of course the skill of the Productives and the Estimator.

This K.P.I is probably more useful in the preparation of budgets and business plans as opposed to measuring the effectiveness of your Productives.

# Retail : Insurance Ratio

## Retail Hours Sold ÷ Insurance Hours Sold

## Guideline: Own Policy

At the time of writing this book, this K.P.I is not evident in any manufacturers composites or financial reports. It provides you with the rate and direction of growth of the Bodyshop by understanding the relationship between the sale of retail hours and insurance hours.

Example:
(A) Retail Hours Sold = 870
(B) Insurance Hours Sold = 1031
(C) **Retail : Insurance Ratio** = **0.84:1**  (A ÷ B)

Recovery Rates from Insurance Companies are often much lower than can be achieved within the retail sector, but once relationships are well established, taking additional insurance work may be the line of least resistance.

If the underlying trend of this K.P.I is demonstrating a higher dependence upon Insurance work, it could mean that your Bodyshop is losing its retail customers, or there are no effective marketing efforts in place to attract retail customers to your business.

Business growth is all well and good, but if most of the growth is from insurance companies you may wish to give some thought to your business's Gross Profitability and exposure. What would happen if an insurance company suddenly decided to place their work elsewhere?

# Revenue per Productive

## Department Turnover ÷ Number of Productives

## Guideline: Own Policy

This is another of those key performance indicators that is used to level the playing field when comparing one business with another.

It removes the emotion of the big numbers that may be involved and produces an average monetary value of Turnover per Productive in any given period.

Example:
(A) Bodyshop Turnover = £573,088
(B) Number of Productives = 6
(C) **Revenue per Productive** = **£95,515** (A ÷ B)

This K.P.I is probably more useful in the preparation of budgets and business plans as opposed to measuring the effectiveness of your Productives.

*Special Note:*
There is a variation across reports with this calculation so be sure that you are measuring the correct statistics.

Some reports class the revenue as Total Department Turnover, whilst others class revenue as the total value of the Hours Sold.

Neither of these statistics is either right or wrong, but do take the time to find out what is included or excluded from your own information.

# Selling Efficiency %

## Hours Worked ÷ Hours Attended (x100)

## Benchmark: 85% - 95%

This K.P.I is also known as Utilisation, Labour Efficiency and Labour Utilisation. The statistic tells you how much of the Productives Attended time is actually spent working productively.

In more simplistic terms, each Productive usually clocks in and is available for eight hours each day, but how much of that time is spent spray-gun-in-hand or panel beating, working on hours that can be charged out to the customer? Selling Efficiency gives you the answer to this question.

Example:
(A) Hours Worked     = 957
(B) Hours Attended    = 1,040
(C) **Selling Efficiency = 92%**   (A ÷ B x 100)

This example shows that the Productives have Attended 1,040 hours at the dealership of which 92% of that time has been spent working productively. The remaining 8% will be shown in your expenses as Idle Time.

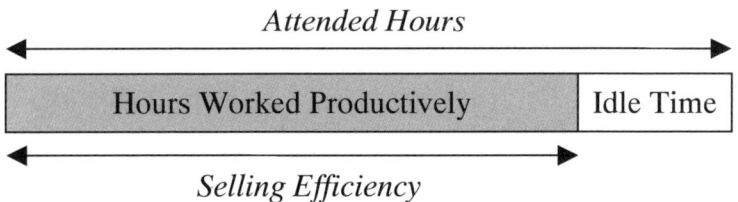

# Semi-Fixed Expenses

## Semi-Fixed Expenses ÷ Total Turnover (x 100)

### Guideline: Own Policy

Semi-Fixed Expenses are those expenses that are not directly linked to the volume of business that you conduct.

They represent those expenses that you have to pay to keep the Bodyshop running whether you repair any vehicles or not.

A good example here is non-productive salaries. If you do not repair any vehicles, you still have to pay the Receptionist, Administrator and Bodyshop Manager.

Example:
(A) Semi-Fixed Expenses    = £143,272
(B) Total Turnover          = £573,088
(C) **Semi-Fixed Expense %** = **25%**   (A ÷ B x 100)

Typically, Semi-Fixed Expenses are shown as a monetary value and in order for you to capture meaningful trend analysis you will need to express them as a percentage of departmental Turnover.

The reason that they are called Semi-Fixed is that they are fixed each month irrespective of sales volume, but the Directors of the business decide at what value those expenses are fixed.

The important thing to note here is that these expenses are <u>not</u> linked to sales volume.

# Utilisation %

**Hours Worked ÷ Hours Attended (x100)**

**Benchmark: 85% - 95%**

This K.P.I is also known as Labour Efficiency, Labour Utilisation and Selling Efficiency. The statistic tells you how much of the Productives Attended time is actually spent working productively.

In more simplistic terms, each Productive usually clocks in and is available for eight hours each day, but how much of that time is spent spray-gun-in-hand or panel beating, working on hours that can be charged out to the customer? Utilisation gives you the answer to this question.

Example:
(A) Hours Worked = 957
(B) Hours Attended = 1,040
(C) **Utilisation** = **92%** (A ÷ B x 100)

This example shows that the Productives have Attended 1,040 hours at the dealership of which 92% of that time has been spent working productively. The remaining 8% will be shown in your expenses as Idle Time.

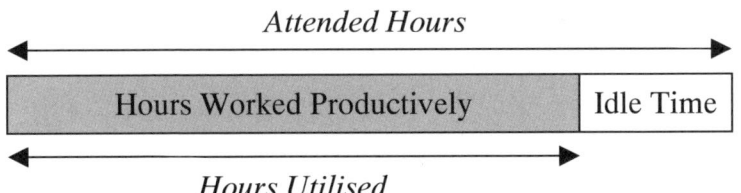

# Variable Expenses

## Variable Expenses ÷ Total Turnover (x 100)

### Guideline: Own Policy

Variable Expenses are those expenses that are directly linked to the volume of business that you conduct. A good example here is consumables. If you do not repair any vehicles then consumables will be zero. As soon as you repair vehicles then consumables build accordingly.

Typically, Variable Expenses are shown as a monetary value and in order for you to capture meaningful trend analysis you will need to express them as a percentage of departmental Turnover.

Example:
(A) Variable Expenses = £18,570
(B) Total Turnover = £371,388
(C) **Variable Expense %** = **5%**   (A ÷ B x 100)

The term "Variable" does not mean that an expense varies by value, nor does it mean that it may change in some way. It simply means that this type of expense grows with the level of business that you conduct.

In order to gain full control over your Departmental Expenses you really need to understand the difference between Variable and Semi-Fixed Expenses and have them separated on your financial reports.

# Vehicle Parc

Your franchise manufacturer provides you with all the vehicles registered within your dealership's area of responsibility over a given period of time; this represents your vehicle parc. These vehicles could be registered by your dealership or by another dealership that is selling vehicles into your area. In many cases the time period for measuring vehicle parc spans 10 years, although this varies from manufacturer to manufacturer.

Example:
Vehicles registered in current year = 958
Vehicles registered in Year 2       = 821
Vehicles registered in Year 3       = 767
Vehicles registered in Year 4       = 789
Vehicles registered in Year 5       = 745
Vehicles registered in Year 6       = 827
Vehicles registered in Year 7       = 754
Vehicles registered in Year 8       = 706
Vehicles registered in Year 9       = 635
Vehicles registered in Year 10      = 582
Total 10-year vehicle parc          = 7,584

In the years that follow, the current vehicle registrations are added and year 10 of the calculation and is replaced with the year 9 statistics and so on, therefore providing a revised ten-year vehicle parc.

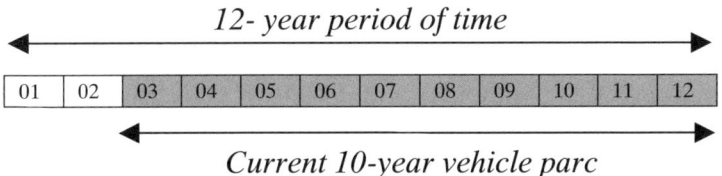

# Working Efficiency %

## Hours Sold ÷ Hours Worked Productively (x100)

### Benchmark: 105% to 115%

This K.P.I. is also known as Productivity and Productive Efficiency. It shows you the Productives ability to complete their work within the agreed hours provided by the Estimator.

This statistic is not as straightforward as the Service Department equation, as due to the nature of the work it is not possible for a franchise manufacturer to apportion standard times.

Example:
(A) Hours Sold = 1,083
(B) Hours Worked productively = 958
(C) **Working Efficiency** = **113%** (A ÷ B x 100)

When a customer brings a vehicle to your Bodyshop for repair you provide them with an estimate that states the number of hours to be charged. This allocated time is the maximum amount that you are able to charge.

In order to make gains in profitability, your Productives must complete the job in a lesser time than is allocated by the Estimator, thereby increasing your Working Efficiency %.

Working Efficiency is a double-edged sword. If you take more time to complete the job then your Working Efficiency falls below 100%.

# Work-In-Progress (Days)

**WIP Hours ÷ N° of Prod's. ÷ Hrs Attended in 1 day**

**Benchmark: 5 days or less**

Work in progress (WIP) simply refers to the number of hours that have been booked onto jobs that have not yet been invoiced.

This vital K.P.I. informs you of the number of days Work In Progress that you have currently accumulated.

Example:
(A) Hours booked as WIP = 216
(B) No of Productives = 6
(C) Hours Attended in 1 day = 8  (Per Productive)
(D) **Work In Progress Days = 4.5 Days**  (A ÷ B ÷ C)

Many financial reports have a tendency to provide WIP as a total monetary value, but this can often be misleading. You must ask the question, is it reporting a value based upon the Labour Cost of Sales, Hours Sold at retail value, or Hours Sold at the current Recovery Rate?

The example above just deals with the number of hours accumulated in WIP and is therefore more useful in trend analysis and deals with all eventualities.

# Interpreting Your Business Information

**Top K.P.I's to study:**

**Net Profit Before Interest %
Circulation of Funds Employed
Return on Funds Employed %
Circulation of Current Assets**

# Absorption % *(Version 1)*

## Aftersales Direct Profit ÷ Total Overheads (x100)

### Baseline: 100% +

The Absorption percentage of a business essentially measures risk. How much of the company's overheads are covered by the profits generated by the Aftersales Departments?

Example:
(A) Direct Profit from Aftersales = £1,154,223
(B) Company Overheads         = £1,452,238
(C) Sales Semi-Fixed Expenses = £189,364
(D) Total Company Overheads   = £1,641,602  (B + C)
(E) **Overhead Absorption**       = **70.31%**  (A ÷ D x 100)
(F) Value of under Absorption = £487,379  (D – A)

This example demonstrates that 70.31% of the overheads are covered by Aftersales, which leaves a shortfall to be recovered by the Sales Department.

Whenever you are measuring the Absorption of your business you should be aware that there are two very different calculations. Basically, the difference between the two calculations lies within the Semi-Fixed Expenses of the Sales Department; some statistics include these expenses whilst others exclude them. This of course makes a considerable difference to the Absorption figure. This version of Absorption is the most accurate, you will understand why when you read version 2.

# Absorption % *(Version 2)*

## Aftersales Direct Profit ÷ Overheads (x100)

### Baseline: 110% +

Absorption was originally set out to measure how much of the company's overheads are being covered by the profits generated from Aftersales, but this second version does not provide you with a truly accurate reflection. This is because the Semi-Fixed Expenses of the Sales Department are omitted from the equation.

Example:
(A) Direct Profit from Aftersales = £1,154,223
(B) Company Overheads = £1,452,238
(C) **Overhead Absorption** = **79.49%** (A ÷ B x 100)
(D) Value of under Absorption = £298,015 (B – A)

This example demonstrates that 79.49% of the overheads are covered by Aftersales, but where are the Semi-Fixed Expenses of the Sales Department?

Some people say that they should be included and some say that they should be excluded. Neither one is right nor wrong, but it does make a big difference to the Absorption percentage. It is all a matter of what you want to measure.

If your financial reports show this version of Absorption then you know that you still have to earn sufficient profit from the Sales Department to cover the Semi-Fixed Expenses. Be sure that you know which version you are using or you could be faced with a sizable shortfall.

# Acid Test *(Version 1)*

## Current Assets – Stock ÷ Current Liabilities (x 100)

### Guideline  Own Policy

The Acid Test of many companies asks this question. If we were to liquidate our Current Assets, would we be able to payoff our short-term debt?

The Acid Test for the motor industry is very subjective as the valuations of our stocks are at the mercy of market forces and people's opinions. For instance, if your used vehicle stock is stated as £250,364 how much could you get for it if you had to liquidate it today?

The same can be said for your Parts stock although most manufactures have a valuation clause within their franchise agreements, typically, this is around 15% below wholesale price of current stock; this usually excludes Obsolete Stock.

Debtors are also subject to scrutiny, how much of your debtors would you be able to recover? You can of course sell your debtors to a factoring company, but this will incur additional costs, usually around 20% of their value.

There are many different calculations for the Acid Test and every company differs depending upon their own particular requirements. Always check the formula for this one to be sure that you know what is being measured.

# Acid Test *(Version 2)*

## Total Assets − Debtors ÷ Total Liabilities (x 100)

### Guideline  Own Policy

This version of the Acid Test measures the balance between the debtors and the rest of the company's investments. The K.P.I. asks the question, if you were to sell all of your Assets today how much money would you be able to recover?

Example:
(A) Total Assets            = £4,623,256
(B) Company Debtors         = £735,994
(C) Assets minus Debtors    = £3,887,262  (A − B)
(D) Total Liabilities       = £4,623,256
(E) **Acid Test**           = **84%**  (C ÷ D x 100)

In this example, the Acid Test shows that if you were able to sell all of your Assets today and recover their stated values, you would be able to cover 84% of your investment; the remaining 16% is tied up in your Debtors.

The equation excludes the value of Debtors because it is unlikely that you would be able to recover all of this money from the people that owe it to you.

The Acid Test is sometimes shown as a ratio as opposed to a percentage. In this instance the reported figure above would be 0.84:1 (C ÷ D)

# Breakeven Volume

## Absorption shortfall ÷ Vehicle Variable Gross Profit

## Baseline: 0 units

This K.P.I. informs you of the number of vehicles that you need to sell to enable your business to reach a point of financial breakeven.

Example:
(A) Direct Profit from Aftersales = £1,154,223
(B) Company Overheads = £1,452,238
(C) Sales Semi-Fixed Expenses = £189,364
(D) Total Company Overheads = £1,641,602 (B + C)
(E) Overhead Absorption = 70.31% (A ÷ D x 100)
(F) **Value of under Absorption** = **£487,379** (D – A)
(G) Variable Gross Profit* = £1,500 per unit
(H) **Vehicle Breakeven Volume = 325 units** (F ÷ G)

This example shows that there is a shortfall in Absorption to the value of £487,379, which means that this business would have to sell 325 units at the average rate of £1,500 Variable Gross Profit per unit to recover this cost at which point your business reaches breakeven.

If Absorption is 100% or higher, then the Vehicle Breakeven Volume is of course zero. However, if Absorption is below 100%, then the shortfall will have to be recovered by the Sales Department.

*Variable Gross Profit is Vehicle Gross Profit less <u>Variable</u> Expenses. Semi-Fixed are contained within the overheads.

# Capital Employed

## Net Worth + Interest-Bearing Borrowings

## Guideline: See Circulation of Funds Employed

Capital Employed is sometimes called Investment or Funds Employed and refers to all of the money that is invested in the company (or nearly all of it).

The total investment is all of the capital that is employed within the company to enable it to operate on a day-to-day basis.

Its constituent parts are Net Worth (the owners funds) and all interest-bearing borrowings. Items such as Creditors, Accruals and the like are excluded from this figure, as they do not attract interest payments.

The value of Capital Employed informs you of how much money is invested into the company to enable it to function on a daily basis and although by itself it is not a K.P.I. it is used in the calculation of many other K.P.I's.

Capital Employed is always shown as a monetary value and is usually shown on the summary page of your financial information. If the value of your Capital Employed is not shown on your summary page you can calculate it for yourself from the Balance Sheet.

Please keep in mind that the value of the Capital Employed is not the same value as the Total Liabilities.

# Cash Profits

## Net Profit After Interest + Depreciation

## Guideline: See Net Profit After Interest

The difference between your company's stated profits and the actual profit you have made is the value of Depreciation.

Depreciation is shown on your Balance Sheet amongst the Fixed Assets and represents the change in value of some or all of your Fixed Assets.

Let's say that you spent £50,000 on equipment last year and its value today, because of wear and tear is now £40,000. In this instance, you new Balance Sheet would show your equipment at £40,000 and Depreciation at £10,000.

This is technically a loss of profit, and therefore your company does not pay tax on Depreciation; naturally, there are laws that state how much Depreciation can be deducted on specific Assets.

Since Depreciation is a paper exercise that reduces your profits, Cash Profit adds back Depreciation to show your true level of profitability and it is this figure that is used to calculate other K.P.I's such as the Loan Repayment %.

# Circulation of Current Assets (C.O.C.A.)

## Annualised Company Turnover ÷ Current Assets

## Baseline: > 12 Times per Annum

At the time of writing this book, this K.P.I is not evident in any manufacturers composites or financial reports. Most organisations measure the effectiveness of the various Stock Turns in each department, but this K.P.I. is the ultimate Stock Turn calculation for your business as a whole.

Example:
(A) Company Turnover = £14,523,661
(B) Current Assets = £1,022,793
(C) **C.O.C.A.** = **14.2 times p/a** (A ÷ B)

The Current Assets of your business contain all of your stocks and therefore this K.P.I. could be viewed as your overall company Stock Turn. The more times you use or circulate your Current Assets, the less money you need to invest in your stocks and therefore the more profit you will make as a direct result.

When you understand the awesome power of this K.P.I. it is surprising that it is not seen in use within the motor industry.

It is often possible to recover more profit through understanding this area of your business than it is from focussing on getting more profit margins from the products and services that you sell so this K.P.I. is worthy of your full consideration.

# Circulation of Funds Employed (C.O.F.E..)

## Annualised Company Turnover ÷ Funds Employed

### Baseline:
**6 times per annum** (if property is on the balance sheet)
**12 times per annum** (if property is not on the balance sheet)

This K.P.I. tells you the number of times that you use, or *circulate* the money that is invested within your dealership in 1 year.

Example:
(A) Company Turnover = £14,523,661
(B) Funds Employed = £2,420,610
(C) **C.O.F.E** = **6 times p/a** (A ÷ B)

C.O.F.E. as it is more commonly known is usually found on the company summary page of your reports and is really a measure of how good your management team are at utilising the funds that are entrusted to them.

It really is true to say that making profit is one thing, but keeping that profit requires a totally different skill.

If you are familiar with stock turn calculations, then this K.P.I. works in exactly the same way except that it is measuring the use of the dealership's money as opposed to the stock in a particular department.

This statistic tells you how many times you use your money in 1 year and the more times you use your money, the less you need to invest and the more profit you will make as a result.

# Current Ratio

## Current Assets ÷ Current Liabilities

### Benchmark: 1.3:1

This K.P.I. informs you whether the value of your Working Capital is enough to service your business. It's rather like the company's blood pressure test.

The calculation for Current Ratio is conducted from the Balance Sheet and is simply Current Assets divided by Current Liabilities.

Example:
(A) Current Assets     = £850,527
(B) Current Liabilities = £654,251
(C) **Current Ratio**     = **1.3:1**  (A ÷ B)

This example is showing a Current Ratio of 1.3:1, which means that for every £1 of Current Liability you have £1.30 in Current Assets.

We need this amount of cover because the nature of our business dictates that our stocks are always suffering the effects of depreciation and as an industry, we have the tendency to pay out money at a faster rate than we receive it.

This K.P.I is also known as the Working Capital Ratio and is one of the most important ratios to monitor to ensure that you have enough cash available on a day-to-day basis to enable your business to function properly.

# Debtor Creditor Ratio

### Debtors ÷ Creditors

### Benchmark:  < 1:1

This K.P.I. measures the amount of money that your customers owe your dealership compared with the amount of money that your dealership owes your suppliers.

Let's say that you sell a product to a customer and they agree to pay you in 30 days time; this is known as a Debtor and is a use of your company's money. A Creditor is the exact opposite of this. You receive products and agree to pay your supplier in 30 days time. The Debtor Creditor Ratio shows the relationship between these two amounts of money.

Example:
(A) Debtors            = £108,182
(B) Creditors          = £135,227
(C) **Debtor Creditor Ratio**  =  0.8:1 (A ÷ B)

As you can see from the example above, on one hand you are loaning money to other companies (Debtors) and on the other hand you are borrowing money from other companies (Creditors).

Generally speaking, it makes good commercial sense to maintain a balance between these two amounts in that they cancel each other out. In any instance, to make your money work smarter, you always need to have more money in Creditors that you have in Debtors thereby showing a ratio of less than 1:1.

# Debtor Days

## Aftersales Debtors ÷ Aftersales Daily Turnover

## Benchmark: < 45 days

The Debtor Days K.P.I is usually a measurement of the credit activity within the Aftersales departments. Its purpose is to inform you of the average number of days that your customers take to pay you.

Example:
(A) Aftersales Debtors = £120,624
(B) Aftersales daily turnover* = £2,805
(C) **Debtor Days** = **43 days** (A ÷ B)

*Note:*
In order to calculate the Aftersales Daily Turnover, you will need to take the annualised Aftersales turnover sold on credit and divide that figure by 365 to arrive at a daily sales turnover.

Example:*
(A) Aftersales Turnover On Credit = £1,023,825
(B) Days in 1 year = 365
(C) Aftersales Daily Credit Turnover = £2,805 (A ÷ B)

In the first example provided above, the average amount of debt is outstanding for a period of 43 days. In many cases, customer credit agreements are for 30 days and all too often these credit terms are not fully instigated and your money is outstanding for longer periods of time. The question is how much longer?

# Debt Equity Ratio

## Total Debt ÷ Net Worth

## Benchmark: < 1.4:1

The Debt Equity Ratio measures how much debt your company has compared to the owners funds. This K.P.I is similar to Gearing, the only difference being that this statistic includes non-interest bearing borrowings such as Creditors and Accruals.

Example:
(A) Total Borrowings = £4,723,161
(B) Net Worth = £5,342,663
(C) **Debt Equity Ratio = 0.88:1** (A ÷ B)

Generally speaking, the value of the owner's funds and the value of borrowed funds is about the same. The Bank Manager may bring more pressure to bare on your company when the Debt Equity Ratio is showing an increasing trend, especially when the ratio is in excess of 1:1. This could mean that the Bank Manager has more money invested in your company than you do, and as you can imagine, they don't like that!

The Debt Equity Ratio is seldom used within the motor industry because Gearing is considered to be a more accurate reflection of the state of the borrowings. This is because some companies are encouraged to increase the values of their Creditors in order to reduce interest-bearing borrowings. In these instances, the Debt Equity Ratio would be unaffected, whilst Gearing would show an improvement.

# Equity %

## Net Worth ÷ Total Liabilities (x100)

## Benchmark: 35%

In simplistic terms this K.P.I tells you how much Equity you have in the business, or in other words, how much of the company belongs to the owners.

Example:
(A) Net Worth       = £1,869,932
(B) Total Liabilities = £5,342,663
(C) **Equity %**    = **35%**   (A ÷ B x 100)

This statistic is used to measure the financial stability of a company and is sometimes used as a measure of the business's ability to borrow money.

If you own your home you will no doubt have heard the term Equity. Let's say that your house is worth £100,000 and you have a mortgage of £75,000. The remaining £25,000 represents the money that you put in to buy your house. This is the part of your house that belongs to you, or in other words this is your Equity.

To calculate your Equity % you simply divide your share (£25,000) by the total value of the house (£100,000) and express this as a percentage (x 100). In this example the Equity that you have in your house would be 25%.

The meaning of Equity in your business is exactly the same and you can find the components for the calculation on your Balance Sheet.

# Fixed Asset %

## Total Fixed Assets ÷ Total Assets (x100)

### Benchmark: 45% to 55%

The primary function of this K.P.I. is to measure the balance between the investment in the facility of the company (land and buildings etc.) and the investment in the day-to-day business that operates within it. In other words, it assesses the balance between long-term and short-term investment.

Example:
(A) Total Fixed Assets = £2,564,478
(B) Total Assets      = £5,342,663
(C) **Fixed Asset %**    = **48%**  (A ÷ B x 100)

This example shows that of all the money that has been spent in your dealership, 48% of the investment is in the facility, and the remaining 52% is invested in stock and all the other things from which you hope to earn profit.

The calculation is taken from the Balance Sheet and is generally shown within the company summary.

The reason for the 10% tolerance in the benchmark is because of the fluctuation in property prices around the country. Therefore an area with high property prices would generate a higher Fixed Asset %.

This K.P.I is only really valid when the land and buildings are shown on the Balance Sheet.

# Funds Employed

## Net Worth + Interest-Bearing Borrowings

### Guideline: See Circulation of Funds Employed

Funds Employed is sometimes called Investment or Capital Employed and refers to all of the money that is invested in the company (or nearly all of it).

The total investment is all of the funds that are employed within the company to enable it to operate on a day-to-day basis.

Its constituent parts are Net Worth (the owners funds) and all interest-bearing borrowings. Items such as Creditors, Accruals and the like are excluded from this figure, as they do not attract interest payments.

The value of Funds Employed informs you of how much money is invested into the company to enable it to function on a daily basis and although by itself it is not a K.P.I. it is used in the calculation of many other K.P.I's.

Funds Employed is always shown as a monetary value and is usually shown on the summary page of your financial information. If the value of your Funds Employed is not shown on your summary page you can calculate it for yourself from the balance sheet.

Please keep in mind that the value of the Funds Employed is not the same value as the Total Liabilities.

# Gearing Ratio

## Interest-Bearing Borrowings ÷ Net Worth

## Benchmark: < 1.4:1

The term gearing is all about the relationship between the level of Equity in a business and the amount of money that is currently being borrowed.

Example:
| | | |
|---|---|---|
| (A) Interest-Bearing Borrowings | = | £4,541,263 |
| (B) Net Worth | = | £5,342,663 |
| (C) **Gearing Ratio** | = | **0.8:1** (A ÷ B) |

Generally speaking, a Bank Manager is relatively happy to maintain Gearing at 1:1. This means that for every £1 that you have invested in the business, the Bank Manager will also invest £1.

When Gearing goes over and above 1:1 this is the time when you may experience increasing pressure from the bank to repay some of your loans. After all, the bank does not want to put more money into your business than you have invested yourself.

There are two different ways of expressing Gearing, this method provides you with a Gearing Ratio; the other provides you with the Gearing %. Although both K.P.I's are called Gearing, they do measure slightly differently.

# Gearing %

**Interest-Bearing Borrowings ÷ Funds Employed x100**

**Benchmark: < 60%**

This version of Gearing measures the relationship between how much of the Funds Employed are owed in interest-bearing borrowings.

Example:
(A) Interest-Bearing Borrowings = £4,541,263
(B) Funds Employed = £9,883,926
(C) **Gearing Percentage** = **46%**  (A ÷ B x 100)

Generally speaking, a Bank Manager is relatively happy to maintain Gearing at 50%. This means that for every £1 that you have invested in the business, the Bank Manager will also invest £1.

Both of these versions of Gearing generate the same answer, albeit in a different way. However, the net result is the same.

The example above is stating that 46% of the money invested in the business is from loans and therefore the remaining 54% is the owner's funds.

# Interest %

## Total Interest ÷ Total Turnover (x 100)

## Benchmark: < 1%

This K.P.I. assesses the level of interest that you are paying and expresses it as a percentage against your company Turnover.

Example:
(A) Annual Interest payments = £101,665
(B) Company Turnover = £14,523,661
(C) **Interest %** = **0.7 %**  (A ÷ B x 100)

The amount of interest that a company is paying on its borrowings is always of primary concern, especially when interest rates are increasing. However, nearly all businesses borrow money at some time so the question must be how much interest is your company paying and is it too much?

It is generally accepted that the level of interest that you are paying should be less than 1% of your company turnover.

If this K.P.I is higher in your business then you may wish to arrange a meeting with your Bank Manager or your other providers of money to renegotiate your terms.

(Also see interest cover)

# Interest Cover

## Total Interest ÷ Cash Profits (x 100)

## Benchmark: < 33%

This K.P.I establishes your total interest payments against the value of your Cash Profits.

When you approach your Bank Manager to borrow money, their concern is whether or not you can afford to pay the interest on your loan, as they usually have your buildings as security against the principal loan value. This is how they assess your business in this area.

Example:
(A) Annual Interest Payments = £90,697
(B) Cash Profits = £412,263
(C) **Interest Cover** = **22 %**  (A ÷ B x 100)

In many cases, your Bank Manager will calculate this figure and if it is less than the guideline of 33% they may ask you if you are borrowing enough money.

Ironically, they do not assess your business's ability to repay the whole of the loan repayment and therefore it is critical that you also calculate the Loan Repayment % for yourself.

(See also Interest %)

# Investment

## Net Worth + Interest-Bearing Borrowings

## Guideline: (See Circulation of Funds Employed)

Investment is sometimes called Funds Employed or Capital Employed and refers to all of the money that is invested in the company (or nearly all of it).

The total investment is all of the funds that are employed within the company to enable it to operate on a day-to-day basis.

Its constituent parts are Net Worth (the owners funds) and all interest-bearing borrowings. Items such as Creditors, Accruals and the like are excluded from this figure, as they do not attract interest payments.

The value of investment informs you of how much money is invested into the company to enable it to function on a daily basis and although by itself it is not a K.P.I. it is used in the calculation of many other K.P.I's.

Investment is always shown as a monetary value and is usually shown on the summary page of your financial information. If the value of your Investment is not shown on your summary page you can calculate it for yourself from the balance sheet.

Please keep in mind that the value of the Investment is not the same value as the Total Liabilities.

# Loan Repayment %

## Annual loan repayment ÷ Cash Profit (x100)

## Benchmark: < 33%

This K.P.I. informs you of how much money your business can afford to repay in annual loan repayments.

Example:
(A) Annual Loan Repayments  = £142,879
(B) Net Profit After Interest  = £508,327
(C) Depreciation  = £87,000
(D) Cash Profits  = £595,327  (B + C)
(E) **Loan Repayment**  = **24 %**  (A ÷ D x 100)

The logic behind this information is rather similar to your mortgage payments. In simplistic terms, a Bank Manager will allow you to borrow somewhere in the region of 3 times your salary for a mortgage.

The company's equivalent to your salary is its Cash Profit and the Loan Repayment % states that the amount that you are paying in loan repayments should be less than one third of your Cash Profits.

To ensure that your business can afford to repay its loans, you may need to restructure them over a longer period of time.

Our usual logic tells that we should pay off our loans in the fastest possible time however, it is better to pay a little more in interest payments than it is to go bust through a lack of cash.

# Net Profit After Interest % (N.P.A.I.)

**Net Profit After Interest ÷ Company Turnover (x 100)**

**Baseline: > 2%**

This is the K.P.I that many franchise manufacturers refer to when discussing levels of profitability within their dealer networks and it is often referred to as the company's bottom line.

Example:
(A) N.P.A.I. = £363,091
(B) Company Turnover = £14,523,661
(C) **N.P.A.I. %** = **2.5%**  (A ÷ B x 100)

Many business owners consider this to be one of the figures that holds the most importance, as it provides you with the profit you have retained as a percentage of the products and services that you have sold.

It is important to keep an eye on the trend of this K.P.I. because a diminishing trend could indicate that you are working harder for a lower return, a condition otherwise known as busy fool syndrome

This K.P.I. is also referred to as Net Profit Before Tax on some financial reports as the only other item to be deducted from this figure is taxation.

This statistic is obviously influenced by Net Profit Before Interest and of course the level of interest that you are paying.

(See also Net Profit Before Interest % and Interest %)

# Net Profit Before Interest % (N.P.B.I.)

## N.P.B.I. ÷ Turnover (x 100)

### Baseline: > 3%

This is probably one of the most important *profit* indicators for a business to measure. It provides you with the dealership result as opposed to an individual departmental result.

Example:
(A) N.P.B.I.           = £508,327
(B) Company Turnover   = £14,523,661
(C) **N.P.B.I. %**     = **3.5%**   (A ÷ B x 100)

The N.P.B.I.% statistic gives you the capability to measure the ability of the company to retain profit from the products and services that it is selling, without taking the cost of capital into account.

This means that you can accurately compare two companies, on a like-for-like basis, without the interference of their financial stability or borrowings. This is critical when you are using Composite comparison.

Without doubt, this KPI is the best measurement when comparing the profitability between companies. It simply states how much of your turnover has been retained as profit. *(Before Interest)*

# Net Profit Before Tax % (N.P.B.T.)

## Net Profit Before Tax ÷ Company Turnover (x 100)

### Baseline: > 2%

This is the K.P.I that many franchise manufacturers refer to when discussing levels of profitability within their dealer networks and it is often referred to as the company's bottom line. It is also known as Net Profit After Interest or Return on Sales.

Example:
(A) N.P.B.T.           = £363,091
(B) Company Turnover   = £14,523,661
(C) **N.P.B.T. %**     = **2.5%**  (A ÷ B x 100)

Many business owners consider this to be one of the figures that holds the most importance, as it provides you with the profit you have retained as a percentage of the products and services that you have sold.

It is important to keep an eye on the trend of this K.P.I. because a diminishing trend could indicate that you are working harder for a lower return, a condition otherwise known as busy fool syndrome

There are no K.P.I measurements for profitability after taxation has been deducted, as the parameters and individual situations for taxation are different for every business.

(See also Net Profit Before Interest %)

# Return on Funds Employed % (R.O.F.E.)

## Value of N.P.B.I. ÷ Funds Employed (x 100)

### Baseline: > 21%

This K.P.I. is also known as Return on Investment and measures the ability of your business to grow from the profits that it generates.

The best time for a business to expand is when this K.P.I is showing an increasing trend in line with the suggested baseline because this means that any growth can be funded by the company's profits as opposed to borrowed funds.

Example:
(A) Net Profit Before Interest = £508,327
(B) Funds Employed = £2,420,610
(C) **Return On Funds Employed** = 21% (A ÷ B x 100)

When anyone sets up a business, the main aim is to generate a profit. Obviously, you need sufficient profit to pay all the bills and salaries with some left over to enable the business to grow in the forthcoming year.

The reason that interest is not shown within this equation is because it measures the amount of profit being generated without any interference of borrowed funds.

If the trend of this K.P.I is diminishing, then you might choose to reconsider your overall business viability, as you will have a greater dependence upon borrowed funds, therefore increasing interest charges and reducing profitability.

# Return on Investment % (R.O.I.)

## Value of N.P.B.I. ÷ Investment (x 100)

### Baseline: > 21%

This K.P.I. is also known as Return on Funds Employed and measures the ability of your business to grow from the profits that it generates.

The best time for a business to expand is when this K.P.I is showing an increasing trend in line with the suggested baseline because this means that the growth can be funded by the company's profits as opposed to borrowed funds.

Example:
(A) Net Profit Before Interest = £508,327
(B) Funds Employed = £2,420,610
(C) **Return On Investment** = **21%** (A ÷ B x 100)

When anyone sets up a business, the main aim is to generate a profit. Obviously, you need sufficient profit to pay all the bills and salaries with some left over to enable the business to grow in the forthcoming year.

The reason that interest is not shown within this equation is because it measures the amount of profit being generated without any interference of borrowed funds.

If the trend of this K.P.I is diminishing, then you might choose to reconsider your overall business viability, as you will have a greater dependence upon borrowed funds, therefore increasing interest charges and reducing profitability.

# Return on Net Worth

## NPBI ÷ Net Worth (x 100)

## Guideline: Own Policy

This K.P.I is also known as Return on Own Funds. The calculation is very similar to Return on Funds Employed excepting that it uses the value of Net Worth as opposed to the total value of Funds Employed.

Example:
(A) Net Profit Before Interest = £508,327
(B) Net Worth = £847,213
(C) **Return On Net Worth = 59.8%**  (A ÷ B x 100)

This figure can in some cases be very misleading as it is based on the value of Net Worth, therefore it is the trend of this K.P.I that is of most value to you.

The danger of too much reliance upon this K.P.I. is that if your value of Net Worth decreases, this percentage figure could be showing an increasing trend.

You should use this information in accordance with your Equity percentage together with your Return on Funds Employed percentage to establish a meaningful cross-reference.

# Return on Own Funds

## N.P.B.I. ÷ Own Funds (x 100)

## Guideline: Own Policy

This K.P.I is also known as Return on Net Worth. The calculation is very similar to Return on Funds Employed excepting that it uses the value of Net Worth as opposed to the total value of Funds employed.

Example:
(A) Net Profit Before Interest = £508,327
(B) Own Funds = £847,213
(C) **Return On Own Funds = 59.8%** (A ÷ B x 100)

This figure can in some cases be very misleading as it is based on the value of the owner's funds, therefore it is the trend of this K.P.I that is of most value to you.

The danger of too much reliance upon this K.P.I. is that if the value of the owner's funds decreases, this percentage figure could be showing an increasing trend.

You should use this information in accordance with your Equity percentage together with your Return on Funds Employed to arrive at a meaningful conclusion.

# Return on Sales % (R.O.S.)

**Net Profit After Interest ÷ Company Turnover (x 100)**

**Baseline: > 2%**

This is the K.P.I that many franchise manufacturers refer to when discussing levels of profitability within their dealer networks and it is often referred to as the company's bottom line.

It is also referred to as Net Profit After Interest or Net Profit Before Tax on some financial reports and the only other item to be deducted from this figure is taxation.

Example:
(A) Net Profit After Interest = £363,091
(B) Company Turnover = £14,523,661
(C) **Return on Sales %** = **2.5%** (A ÷ B x 100)

Many business owners consider this to be one of the figures that holds the most importance, as it provides you with the profit you have retained as a percentage of the products and services that you have sold.

It is important to keep an eye on the trend of this K.P.I. because a diminishing trend could indicate that you are working harder for a lower return, a condition otherwise known as busy fool syndrome.

This statistic is obviously influenced by Net Profit Before Interest and of course the level of interest that you are paying.

(See also Net Profit Before Interest % and Interest %)

# Working Capital

## Current Assets − Current Liabilities

## Benchmark: See Current Ratio

Working Capital is the value of money that is used to run your business on a day-to-day basis. It's the money that is invested within the part of your business where you buy and sell your products and services. Working capital is not contained within your property or any other Fixed Assets.

The calculation for Working Capital is conducted from the Balance Sheet and is simply Current Assets minus Current Liabilities. This will provide you with the value of Working Capital currently available.

Example:
(A) Current Assets     =    £850,527
(B) Current Liabilities   =    £654,251
(C) **Working Capital   =    £196,276**   (A - B)

However, this equation does not inform you of whether the value of Working Capital is sufficient to sustain the business on a day-to-day basis.

If your business were a human body, then cash would be its blood. You need just the right amount to sustain life; too much and you might cause a haemorrhage, too little and you die.

To assess whether you have just the right amount, you need to calculate the Current Ratio or Working Capital Ratio.

# Working Capital Ratio

## Current Assets ÷ Current Liabilities

## Benchmark: 1.3:1

This K.P.I. informs you whether the value of your Working Capital is enough to service your business. It's rather like the company's blood pressure test.

The calculation for Working Capital Ratio is conducted from the Balance Sheet and is simply Current Assets divided by Current Liabilities.

Example:
(A) Current Assets = £850,527
(B) Current Liabilities = £654,251
 (C) **Working Capital Ratio = 1.3:1** (A ÷ B)

This example is showing a Working Capital Ratio of 1.3:1, which means that for every £1 of current liability you have £1.30 in Current Assets.

We need this amount of cover because the nature of our business dictates that our stocks are always suffering the effects of depreciation and as an industry, we have the tendency to pay out money at a faster rate than we receive it.

It is also known as the Current Ratio and is one of the most important ratios to monitor to ensure that you have enough cash available on a day-to-day basis to enable your business to function properly.

# Conclusion

Modern life is different from any earlier time. Because of the remarkable technological advances, information comes at us from every angle and alternative business strategies are more prevalent.

The key to success is measuring the effects of our business decisions and responding to them quickly in order to enhance profitability.

Without question, the quickest and most stable way to assess our business strategies is by the use of Key Performance Indicators.

In writing this book, I have endeavoured to capture every Key Performance Indicator within the motor industry. With the best of intentions providing me with direction, I ventured forward to break down the barriers of industry jargon to produce a book that I hope you have found to be easy to understand and above all, useful.

During the compilation of the data, I found a few K.P.I's that drifted into the realms of analysis paralysis, in other words, they exist, but no one knows why! For the sake of maintaining usefulness (and my own sanity) I have chosen to omit these statistics from the book.

If you are in possession of Key Performance Indicators that you find useful which are not included within this book, then please forward them on to me together with your thoughts and I'll be delighted to include them in the second edition.

Now that you have your own copy of The K.P.I Book, what about every other manager in your business?

***"It's not companies who are successful...
It's the people working within them."***

Naturally, you will want to keep your copy of The K.P.I. Book to yourself for safe keeping so that you know where to find it at that critical time when you need it.

The day you stop learning is the day you stop earning, and this is true for all managers in business. By investing in The K.P.I. Book for all your management team you are investing in the people who will be making sure that your company is successful in the future.

To order by telephone in the UK:
01384 371432

To order by telephone outside of the UK:
0044 1384 371432

Email: KPI@AskInsight.com

Visit our web site: www.AskInsight.com

Insight Training & Development Ltd
Publications Department
P. O. Box 1234
Stourbridge
England
DY8 2GE